kid
chef
Every Day

kid chef Every Day

The EASY COOKBOOK FOR FOODIE KIDS

SIMPLE RECIPES AND ESSENTIAL TECHNIQUES
TO WOW YOUR FAMILY

Colleen Kennedy

Photography by Evi Abeler

ROCKRIDGE
PRESS

Cover Designer: William Mack
Interior Designer: Emma Hall
Editors: Meg Ilasco and Lia Brown
Production Editor: Erum Khan
Cover and Interior Photography © 2018 Evi Abeler. Food styling by Albane Sharrard.
Author photo © Kara Raudenbush Photography

ISBN: Print 978-1-64152-222-9 | eBook 978-1-64152-223-6

Anyone can cook;
they just have to *want* to.
Here's to YOU spending more
time in the kitchen cooking
and baking up delicious
memories!

CONTENTS

·····························

INTRODUCTION

If you are reading this, you most likely have a special interest in cooking or baking and are ready to take your skills to the next level. That's awesome! My hope is that this book will help propel you to become a confident home cook who can make an ever-expanding variety of dishes.

When you really get to know your way around the kitchen and are not afraid to try new recipes, you will become known by your family and friends as "the one who makes all the delicious foods." How cool is that? Plus, there is nothing more satisfying than wanting to eat something specific and being able to stroll into your kitchen and whip it up all by yourself!

I received my first cookbook the Christmas I was nine years old. I almost immediately read it from cover to cover. The very next day, I made my first recipe from the book. Of all the things in the world I could have made, I made a chocolate cake with chocolate icing covered in popcorn (yes, popcorn!). It was called a Blizzard Cake. What I remember most about making that cake was not the actual making of the cake but what happened next.

As I carried that cake out to my brothers, sister, parents, and grandmother, all eyes were on me. I felt proud. I felt confident. I felt important. That was the moment I fell in love with cooking. I wanted to have those feelings again and again and again. I realized that the simple act of me being excited about cooking made other people happy, and in return, that made me happy.

I hope that by exploring this book and its countless tips and recipes, you'll blossom into a confident, skilled Kid Chef who has everyone in your social circle excited to see what you cook up next!

PART ONE

Cooking Class

You can probably already envision your first recipe. But before you start cracking those eggs, let's walk together through some of the information you'll want to know as you advance your skills. These are the things that will make the cooking process easier, and they may even mean the difference between a culinary feat and a flop. I promise you'll learn things that will one day leave you saying "I'm so glad I knew that!"

your kitchen

In this chapter, you will find the rules, the tools, the tips, and the tricks that will help enhance your emerging skills as an adventurous home cook and set you up for new achievements in the kitchen. Ready to level up and wow your family and friends? Let's go!

RULES FOR SUCCESSFUL COOKING

These rules may not be like the ones you have in school. Although some rules are safety-minded, others are more about helping you work smarter, not harder. Even the cooking pros on TV will tell you about the times they didn't read a recipe all the way through and had to stop everything and run out to get one missing ingredient.

1. **Check in with an adult.** Every family has different rules when it comes to young adults cooking. Check in with an adult before you begin. Show them the recipe you plan to make, and decide together if there are any steps or tools that you may need help or guidance with.

2. **Read the recipe, *twice*.** Always read through the recipe you are planning to make at least twice before you begin. Knowing exactly what ingredients, tools, and steps are involved will lead to a smoother cooking experience.

3. **Get organized.** It's easy to set yourself up for success in the kitchen; just be as organized as you can before you begin cooking or baking a dish. Prepping your ingredients ahead of time and cleaning up along the way is the way to go. The next two tips offer some best practices in these areas for every home cook.

4. **Prep ahead of time.** Before you shop for ingredients for a recipe, do a quick inventory of your pantry, refrigerator, spice cabinet, and/or garden to see what you already have. Next, make a list of what you need. Then double-check that list—it's no fun when you're making a dish and suddenly realize you are missing an ingredient.

> ## KID CHEF TIPS
>
> Watch videos of celebrity chefs and their techniques. Whether it's the way they chop an onion or get the perfect sear on a steak, you will be amazed what you can learn!

5. **Set the stage.** Picture your favorite TV chef. What does their work space look like? Things like keeping a clean work surface and measuring ingredients in advance are rules you'll want to make for yourself (see 8 Tips for the Organized Chef, page 17).

6. **Do one job at a time.** Cooking requires concentration, especially as you are learning. Cooking more than one dish at a time is like juggling. You will master it; it just takes some practice. Start slowly, and work your way toward more complex tasks.

7. **Clean as you go.** Put away ingredients or tools when you are finished with them. Clean up spills right away.

8. **Wash produce.** Always wash your fruits and vegetables with clean hands or a clean vegetable brush, even if you're planning to peel them. When you cut produce with a knife, the knife transfers whatever grime and bacteria was outside to the inside. Dry clean produce with a clean cloth or paper towel. Remove and discard the outermost layers of lettuce, cabbage, and Brussels sprouts.

9. **Remember hand washing.** You'll always want to start with clean hands and wash your hands with warm soapy water whenever you touch raw meat, meat juices, raw eggs, fresh produce, or dirty dishes. Oh, and of course anytime you happen to sample your products mid-recipe.

10. **Be electric safe.** Reduce the risk of electric shock by keeping any electric kitchen tools and small appliances away from water.

11. **Be knife safe.** Always be aware when you have a knife in your hand, especially if you have younger siblings in your house. Don't suddenly turn around with it in your hand. When you're not using it, put it down and make sure it is out of reach of younger children.

12. **Be heat safe.** Always use oven mitts and pot holders. To remind yourself that a pan is hot from the oven, lean an oven mitt on it or slide it onto the handle after you remove it from the oven. When you are finished with the oven or other kitchen appliances, turn them off.

THE ONLY EQUIPMENT YOU NEED

From muffin pans to Microplanes, the right tools are essential for successful cooking results. Take a look at the following descriptions so you'll be familiar with the equipment used in each recipe:

COOKWARE & BAKEWARE

 Baking dishes or casseroles Deep dishes in various shapes and sizes, used for baking and roasting.

 Baking sheets Large trays (preferably rimmed to avoid dripping), used for baking, roasting, and cooking.

 Muffin pans Baking pans with built-in cups; they come in both regular size (12 cups) and mini (24 cups).

 **Saucepan** A deep pan, used for boiling, simmering, and searing.

 Skillet or sauté pan A shallow pan used for sautéing, frying, and more. Cast-iron skillets are preferable as they cook evenly and are oven-safe and excellent for searing.

 Springform pan A round cake pan with a removable bottom. It's ideal for baking dishes like cheesecake and quiches, foods with delicate contents that don't allow you to invert them. It cannot be used to bake thin batters, as they will leak out of the pan's seams.

 Wire cooling rack A flat wire grid with feet that allows baked goods to rest and cool and prevents them from getting soggy with condensation.

TOOLS & UTENSILS

 Chef's knife Versatile cutting, dicing, slicing, and chopping tool with a blade and handle.

 Colander A bowl with holes, used to drain pasta, strain food from liquids, and clean fruits and vegetables.

 Cutting boards A flat platform for slicing, chopping, dicing, etc., usually made of plastic or wood. Separate cutting boards are recommended for produce and proteins (meats, poultry, and fish).

Grater A tool with many small blades on the surface, used to grate cheese, vegetables, and more.

 Measuring cups Glass measuring cups used for liquid measuring, and metal or plastic measuring cups for dry measuring.

 Measuring spoons Metal or plastic spoons that measure both liquid and dry ingredients.

 Meat thermometer You'll want one of these to make sure your meats are cooked to the correct temperature (see chart, page 29).

 Microplane or zester A tool that removes fine shreds of zest (or peel) from citrus fruit.

 Mixing bowls Bowls in various sizes used for mixing ingredients.

 Oven mitts Heat-safe mittens for handling hot cookware and bakeware.

 Paring knife A small-bladed knife for peeling and working with small vegetables and fruits.

 Spatulas Tools with a handle and scraping edge. Metal spatulas are used for lifting foods off trays and flipping food on hot surfaces, and plastic or silicone spatulas are used for mixing or handling food on a nonstick surface.

 Whisk A tool with a handle and wire loops, used to incorporate air into wet ingredients and help make a sauce or gravy smooth.

SMALL APPLIANCES

 Blender or immersion blender A mixing device used to blend liquids, purée foods, and more. An immersion blender is a handheld mixer that is submerged in the food before you turn it on.

 Food processor An appliance similar to a blender, but with a wider basin, used for chopping or mincing foods.

 Stand or hand mixer An appliance with blades for mixing batter and dough, and for making whipped cream, frosting, and more.

STOCKING YOUR SHELVES

The key to many successful meals is the quality of certain ingredients. As you gain experience, you will learn which ingredients are worth splurging on and which ones you don't have to. The following ingredients are those you'll want to have on hand for a variety of recipes and uses.

Pantry Essentials

Baking staples White and brown sugar, honey, flour, vanilla extract, ground cinnamon, nutmeg, raisins, chocolate chips, baking soda (replace every 3 months), baking powder, and old-fashioned rolled oats are staples for many delicious baking recipes.

Fresh herbs Parsley, cilantro, mint, oregano, sage, and thyme give dishes an amazing boost of fresh flavor. Dried herbs can often be substituted, but fresh usually tastes more vibrant.

Garlic Fresh garlic is great; however, I swear by garlic paste for many of the recipes I make. It's packed just after it's harvested, it won't burn and turn bitter like minced garlic can if you are not careful, it has incredible flavor, plus it saves time and makes no mess! Refrigerated jarred garlic is fine, but stay away from non-refrigerated chopped or minced garlic—they're not nearly as flavorful.

Grains Keep pasta, rice, oats, and bread crumbs on hand—you'll find many uses for them in recipes.

Oils There are many healthy oils you can use that are great for cooking. Some people bake almost exclusively with coconut oil, which is solid until it melts. For some it's only olive oil, while others experiment with a variety of oils. I choose to use grapeseed oil for most of my dressings and marinades and for sautéing, since it's flavorless and has a high smoke point (meaning it can stand up to heat better than other oils). When I need to drizzle oil onto cheese, hummus, or salads, I grab olive oil for the nice flavor it imparts.

Scallions and onions Did you know that onions are the most consumed vegetable in the world? (Second is the potato.) Surprising, since people are not strolling around crunching on them like apples! Instead,

onions and scallions are used behind the scenes, in stocks and marinades and with meats and other veggies, to lend excellent flavor and depth.

Seasonings Salt, freshly ground black pepper, garlic powder, onion powder, ground cayenne (red) pepper, Cajun seasoning, blackening seasoning, and soy sauce are all used often in cooking. My rule of thumb for salt is this: When baking, use table salt; when cooking, use kosher salt. Sea salt and other artisanal salts are typically used for finishing a dish just before serving. But they're all nice to have.

Stock Always have store-bought or homemade chicken or vegetable stock on hand for soups, dips, and more. This liquid is made from cooking bony parts. Broth, a thinner liquid made from cooking meat, is a good substitute, but stock has a richer flavor.

Refrigerator Essentials

Butter There is nothing quite like butter for adding flavor and richness to recipes. If you like baking, you'll always want to have butter on hand. Unsalted butter is usually used for baking, and salted for nearly everything else. When butter is called for in recipes, use stick butter rather than whipped.

Buttermilk This ingredient adds moisture and depth to quick breads, cakes, and biscuits, and when making fried chicken it's a must. No buttermilk? No problem; just substitute 1 cup of milk with 1 tablespoon of fresh lemon juice, stir, and let it sit for 5 minutes.

Cheese Typically, block cheese is best—it tends to melt better, and pre-shredded varieties usually contain additives. When a recipe calls for Parmesan or another hard cheese, shred or grate it yourself (and enjoy a piece or two while you do!). For some things, like a dip or wrap sandwich, buying pre-shredded works fine. Same goes for soft cheese like feta or goat cheese; it's best if you purchase a small log and crumble it yourself.

Eggs Used both for cooking and baking, eggs are an important kitchen staple. Always make sure you have eggs on hand.

Heavy cream You can make homemade whipped cream with a bit of powdered sugar and a hand mixer in 3 to 4 minutes, and it tastes so much better than store-bought. Keep it on hand to perk up pies, smoothies, ice cream, and cake.

Lemons and limes The juice and zest from these citrus fruits adds special flavor and acidity to recipes.

Pizza dough If you want to make it, go right ahead. I choose to buy it for $2.50 from my local pizza shop. It's fresh and they make it all day long, and much better than I can. Best deal ever! No cleanup and it's always perfect.

DON'T WASTE . . . COOK ECO-FRIENDLY!

The amount of food waste in the United States alone is enormous, but you can make such a difference. Here are some suggestions for reducing waste:

- What's left of an ingredient, and what can you use it for? For example, keep a freezer-safe container nearby for the ends of onions (including skins), carrots, left-over herbs, or parts of garlic heads. Freeze the bag and keep it for making stocks or broths. You can always freeze stock for later use.

- Have leftover tomato paste? Freeze it in an ice cube tray for the next time you need a tablespoon or two.

- Freeze the end of Parmesan rinds to throw into homemade pasta sauce for extra richness.

- Chicken carcass, skins, and beef bones are all great to make stock from.

- Find some wilted veggies in the fridge? Plunk them in a bowl of ice water; they may perk up. If not, use them for stock.

- Have a one- or two-day-old piece of fresh baked bread? Run the bread under water for just a second, place it right on the rack in a 325°F oven for 6 to 10 minutes, and ta-dah! Your bread is no longer stale.

- Use plastic storage bags and paper towels sparingly.

- While prepping and cooking, be aware of how much water you're using. Don't let the sink run continuously; only turn the water on when you need it. When you have a bowlful of water from washing fruits or vegetables, take it outside and water the plants.

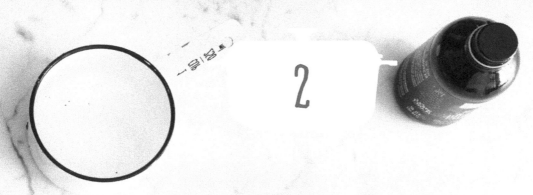

everyday kitchen skills

Let's talk about some of the essential skills and how-tos every home cook needs to know. From knife skills, to working with ingredients, to the various ways you can use your oven and stove, the following tips and techniques will help you in your culinary journey.

REVIEW THE BASICS

When it comes to cooking, the more organized you are, typically the more successful you will be. Check out these tips to prep and cook like a pro.

Reading a Recipe

It is so exciting to take a pile of ingredients and transform them into a finished dish! However, understanding a recipe before you begin is the most important step.

Read the whole recipe, two or three times. Relax, sit down, and *really* read the recipe through. Pay attention to the order of the recipe. It's usually written that way for a reason.

Recipes are broken down into components. Reading, understanding, preparing for, and following the various parts of a recipe are what set you up for success. Here are all the parts of a recipe:

Recipe Title: The recipe title is a good indicator of what to expect from a recipe.

Recipe Yield: The yield or number of servings in a recipe helps you understand how many people it will feed and is a great indicator of whether you should double or even halve the recipe to meet your needs.

Ingredients: The list of ingredients and their corresponding amounts and measurements set the tone for how the recipe will flow. Typically ingredients are listed in the order of their use. Setting out your ingredients prior to beginning a recipe is a pro tip. Once you think you are finished prepping a recipe, read the ingredient list again make sure you remembered all the ingredients.

Instructions/Directions: The instructions or directions of a recipe are the steps you need to take to create a chosen recipe.

Equipment/Tools Needed: The equipment/tools needed section is there for you to set out most of what you'll need to cook or bake a recipe.

> ### KID CHEF TIPS
> Never be caught without butter again. Butter freezes great, so pop a pound in the freezer for those uh-oh moments.

CHEF LINGO

The culinary world has a language all its own. Start getting acquainted with some of the terms; it'll come in handy when they pop up in recipes (and you'll sound so knowledgable when discussing a good dredging!).

Blend To combine separate ingredients into one.

Dash Equal to 2 pinches; considered to be about 1/8 of a teaspoon or less. I use a thumb and three fingers to grab it.

Divided When an ingredient is used in more than one step in a recipe. For example, if a recipe calls for 3 tablespoons butter, divided, you may use 1 tablespoon in the beginning of the recipe and 2 tablespoons in a later step.

Dredge To coat something in flour or bread crumbs.

Emulsify To combine ingredients of different thicknesses, such as oil and vinegar.

Grate Using a grater to break down a solid piece of food, such as cheese, into much smaller, crumb-like pieces.

Incorporate To combine ingredients until they are well blended and evenly distributed.

Marinate Allowing meats, poultry, seafood, or vegetables to sit in a liquid mixture and absorb the flavors.

Mix To stir ingredients until combined.

Pinch Typically 1/16 of a teaspoon or less. Use a thumb and pointer finger to grab a tiny amount of seasoning to add to a dish.

Prep To prepare ingredients or equipment as a recipe directs before using them, such as greasing a pan or chopping.

Season to taste To add as little or as much seasoning to a dish as you prefer.

Shred To tear or cut into long, narrow pieces. Examples of shreddable foods would include chicken or lettuce.

Substitute To swap an ingredient for another ingredient.

Sweat To cook vegetables over medium heat in a small amount of fat (oil/butter) until tender or translucent.

Whip To beat rapidly with a whisk (or by mixer), adding air to whipped cream or an egg white, for example, until it expands.

Working the dough Similar to kneading, this involves pressing and flipping the dough a bit to get a desired consistency.

Zest To remove just the outermost colored layer of a citrus fruit, such as a lemon, lime, or orange, using a Microplane or zester.

Temperature and Time: Typically in the first step of a recipe, it tells you if you need to preheat your oven and if so to what temperature. Additionally, stove-top recipes will tell you in various steps how high to set the stove and how long to cook or bake a recipe. Sometimes the time stated is a guide due to oven temperatures and proteins (meats/poultry/seafood) varying in size and weight.

Notes/Add-Ins: When you come across a section of a recipe called Pro Tip, Try Instead, Helpful Hint, or something similar, that is where suggestions for changes, additional spins on a recipe, or troubleshooting tips are explained.

Measuring Skills

Dry and liquid measuring cups vary from one another. The difference is not enormous; however, each measure was designed to measure wet or dry as precisely as you can get without using a kitchen scale. Using the right cups is more important when it comes to baking versus cooking, since baking is a more precise science.

Dry Measure Dry measuring cups come in stackable sets (¼, ⅓, ½, and 1 cup). When measuring dry ingredients, the dip and sweep method works best. Dip your measuring cup into your dry ingredient, such as flour, sugar, or grain, fill it all the way until it is overflowing (don't pat it down), and then, using the flat side of a butter knife, "sweep" off the excess, leaving your measuring cup filled and level. Brown sugar is the exception—you can pack down this dense, sticky ingredient into the measuring cup.

Liquid Measure Liquid measuring cups are typically transparent and have a spout for easy pouring. When measuring liquids, place your liquid measuring cup on a flat surface (don't hold it in your hand) and pour the liquid in until it looks like it's just under the line of the amount you need. Then squat down and look at it from eye level. Adjust so you have the amount right on the line.

Measuring spoons measure small amounts of both liquid and dry ingredients interchangeably.

8 TIPS FOR THE ORGANIZED CHEF

Here's a term to remember: *mise en place*. Pronounced "meeez on ploss," this is the French culinary term for "everything in its place." Both top chefs and home cooks know that in order to cook smoothly and success-fully, you need to gather your tools and have them in place before you begin. Consider these tips:

1 **Clear the area.** Always start with a clean, clear work space—it will make your job easier.

2 **Gather your tools.** Set out all the ingredients and equipment you will need in advance.

3 **Stand it up.** Prop up your cookbook, tablet, or phone for easy reading of the recipe.

4 **Secure your cutting board.** Put a damp dish towel under your cutting board to keep it still while you slice, dice, and chop.

5 **Spoon, scoop, and chop.** Measure out your ingredients in advance, and then put the rest away.

6 **Keep a garbage bowl nearby.** If you compost or have a garbage disposal, keep two bowls on hand, one for food waste and one for non-food waste.

7 **Wipe smartly.** Tie an apron on or tuck a dish towel into your waistband to wipe your hands on.

8 **Clean along the way.** Keep a clean work space, and place dirty dishes in the sink or dishwasher as you go.

chocolate & peanut butter energy balls

PREP TIME
10 minutes, plus 30 minutes to chill

SERVES

4

3 ENERGY BALLS PER SERVING

TOOLS/ EQUIPMENT

Food processor or blender

Large bowl

Mixing spoon or spatula

1 cup rolled oats

⅓ cup mini chocolate chips

½ cup peanut butter (smooth or crunchy)

¼ cup honey

½ teaspoon vanilla extract

Chop the oats.
In a food processor or blender, pulse or blend the oats until they are a quarter of their original size.

Mix the dough.
Pour the oats into a large bowl, add the chocolate chips, peanut butter, honey, and vanilla, and mix until blended and smooth.

Shape and chill.
Refrigerate the mixture for 30 minutes or more. Form into walnut-sized balls. Store in a covered container in your refrigerator until ready to enjoy.

 TRY INSTEAD Allergic to nuts? You can substitute sunflower butter for the peanut butter.

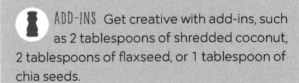 ADD-INS Get creative with add-ins, such as 2 tablespoons of shredded coconut, 2 tablespoons of flaxseed, or 1 tablespoon of chia seeds.

KNIFE SKILLS

Home cooks use a variety of knives. Your main knife is your BFF in the kitchen. A good knife is cherished by both professionals and home chefs alike. The three knives most used by home cooks are a chef's knife, a paring knife, and a bread knife. When your ingredients are cut properly, they will cook uniformly. When raw ingredients are cut well, they look more attractive in their presentation of salads, salsa, garnishes, etc. Best of all, a good knife makes quick work of cutting—have you ever tried cutting with a dull knife? Not fun!

Learning to Cut

Always respect any knife you use. Knives are serious instruments that need to be held and used properly. Always get permission, keep your knives far from the reach of younger kids, and make it a habit never to walk around with a knife in your hand as you move about the kitchen.

KID CHEF TIPS

Sometimes scissors work better than knives. A pair of kitchen shears or clean scissors can be used to cut herbs, scallions, and even shellfish such as crab legs.

How you hold your knife is important. When you hold and move your knife properly, it does the work for you, making your job easier. The knife you will use most when cooking is a chef's knife. You can cut just about anything with it. Here's how to use it: Pick up the knife. Do you see where the blade meets the handle? Take your thumb and your pointer finger and "pinch" the metal where it meets the handle. Wrap your other fingers and hand around the handle. Relax your grip a bit, and let your knife do the work.

Paring knives are small and used when working with certain fruits and veggies like strawberries—use this knife to remove the stem from the strawberry and chop the fruit. Many people prefer to use a paring knife to peel their potatoes and apples instead of an actual peeler.

When it comes to slicing bread or cutting into homemade quick breads, a bread knife does the job best. Its serrated edge makes quick work of slicing rolls and crusty breads. Many bakers like this knife for slicing cakes horizontally (to make additional layers) and for cutting and serving slices, since it produces fewer crumbs.

Now that we've discussed the knives cooks use the most, let's talk about your free hand. This hand is very important when it comes to culinary prep work. It guides whatever you are cutting. You always want to pay attention to what each hand is doing. The hand with the knife is the star of the show, but your other hand is the supporting actor or actress. When you're slicing, dicing, chopping, or mincing, your other hand and fingers should be curled like a bear claw, holding onto whatever it is you are working on, and slowly guiding it toward your knife. This hand position will help protect your fingers from accidents.

Remember to wash and dry your produce before you begin slicing, dicing, and chopping.

How to Slice/Dice an Onion

Slicing an onion For slices, simply halve the onion stem to stem and place one half, flat-side down, on a cutting board. Cut one stem off, leaving the other stem to hold the onion together while you work. Press down on the top of the onion firmly with your fingers and begin slicing your way back to the stem using firm, even strokes. This gives you half-moon slices perfect for sandwiches, peppers and onions, and more.

Dicing an onion Cutting a round onion into small squares may seem like a challenge, but there's a good method. First, halve it stem to stem. Place one half, flat-side down, on a cutting board. Cut one stem off of each half, leaving the other stem to hold the onion together while you work, then peel the onion. Press down on the top of the onion firmly with your fingers, and make 3 or 4 horizontal slices all the way through to just before the stem. Turn the onion and make as many horizontal cuts as you can with the tip of your knife. Space your cuts apart evenly so you end up with an even dice. Turn your onion again, place your "bear claw" fingertips on the back half of the onion, and begin slicing toward the stem, moving your opposite hand backward as you do.

How to Slice/Dice a Tomato

Slicing a tomato You'll want to use a serrated knife, which has a jagged edge. Use a small paring knife to remove the stem. To do this, place your thumb about an inch down from the tip of the knife. Insert the knife tip into the tomato up to your thumb next to the stem, press your thumb on the stem, and move your knife around in a circle. Pop out the stem. Place the tomato on a cutting board, stem-side down. Cut the tomato in half, place the flat side down, and with the tip of your knife, cut right through the tomato, creating half-moon slices.

Dicing a tomato Stand your tomato up with the stem on top. Cut off the two fattest "cheeks" of the tomato, leaving the stem area intact. Spin the tomato around and cut the other two cheeks off, leaving a column where the stem begins. Discard that part. Cut each cheek lengthwise into ¼-inch-wide strips. Cut the strips into a ¼-inch dice.

KID CHEF TIPS

Sharp knives equal safer knives. It's true! Dull knives make you work harder and can slip easily when you are cutting food. Learn to use a knife steel, sharpening stone, or knife sharpener to keep edges sharp.

CUTTING STYLES

There are dozens of ways to cut ingredients. Here are some of the basics:

1 **Dice** To cut a food into similarly sized small cubes more precisely than chopping to ensure even cooking.

2 **Chop** To cut a vegetable or fruit into bite-size or smaller pieces.

3 **Mince** To cut a food into very small pieces. If you chop a vegetable, you can then mince it by cutting it again and again, cutting it smaller with each pass.

4 **Slice** To cut vegetables, fruits, meats, or breads into thin, similarly sized pieces.

5 **Halve** To cut a vegetable or fruit down the middle, resulting in two evenly sized pieces.

PREP TIME
15 minutes

COOK TIME
10 minutes
(optional)

SERVES
4

**TOOLS/
EQUIPMENT**
Cutting board
Knife
Medium bowl
Baking sheet
(optional)
Small bowl

1 pint grape tomatoes

1 large garlic clove, minced

2 tablespoons chopped red onion

½ cup minced mozzarella cheese ball

2 tablespoons chopped fresh basil

½ teaspoon red wine vinegar

½ tablespoon olive oil

Kosher salt

Freshly ground black pepper

1 loaf French bread

Prep and mix the bruschetta.
Dice the tomatoes and transfer to a medium bowl. Add the garlic, onion, mozzarella, basil, vinegar, and oil, season with salt and pepper, and toss to combine.

Prepare the bread.
Slice the French bread. If desired, toast for 5 to 8 minutes on a baking sheet in a 425°F oven to crisp up.

Assemble the dish.
Pack the bruschetta mixture into a small bowl, just big enough to hold it. Press it down just a bit. Invert the bowl onto a serving dish to create a mound of bruschetta. Surround with the bread slices and serve immediately.

TRY INSTEAD If you don't have bread on hand, serve this bruschetta with flatbread crackers, water crackers, or matzah. You can also enjoy this on its own as a salad. It makes a great topping for boneless chicken breasts, too.

PRO TIP You can give toasted French bread more flavor. Before you bake it, brush both sides with olive oil and sprinkle with a little salt, pepper, and parsley. Bake for 6 to 9 minutes. These giant "croutons" are great on soup, too.

HOW TO SAUTÉ AND PAN FRY

Mastering the art of sautéing and pan frying your food might sound fancy, but it's not difficult and is a skill every home cook should have. A hot pan does wonders to proteins and veggies by sealing in their natural juices, intensifying flavors, and producing a beautiful crust. Both of these techniques are easy; they just take a little practice.

Prepping Your Ingredients

In sautéing and pan frying, things move quickly. You'll want to have your ingredients measured out and ready within reach. The more equal in size your cut ingredients are, the better your dish will taste as pieces will cook evenly. That is especially true when it comes to proteins (beef, poultry, pork, and seafood). The larger and thicker each piece is, the longer it will take to cook.

To sauté, you only need a minimal amount of fat, such as butter, oil, or bacon drippings. Choose flavorless oils with higher smoke points, like light olive oil, grapeseed oil, and canola oil. (Save the extra-virgin olive oil for dressings and drizzles.)

For shallow pan frying, choose vegetable oil. You'll need more oil to get the job done, and vegetable oil is less expensive than others.

> ### KID CHEF TIPS
>
> When sautéing or pan frying, don't overcrowd the pan. Veggies and proteins will cook more evenly and be crisp (not soggy) if you leave room, plus they'll be much easier to turn. Cook in batches.

Stove Basics

Whether you are using a gas stove or an electric stove, you'll want to understand your stove top's heat settings. Most stoves differ, so experimenting will help you figure out your best go-to settings.

Low Best for keeping in moisture when cooking. Great for cooking eggs, melting chocolate, and simmering foods.

Medium Used to sauté and brown meats and sauté or "sweat" vegetables like onions, peppers, and garlic. (Sweating veggies releases their

OTHER STOVE TECHNIQUES

Here are some additional terms that describe common cooking styles, both on the stove and in the oven:

Bake To cook foods inside the oven at a constant temperature, which cooks them from the outside.

Blanch To submerge food (typically vegetables) in boiling water for just a few minutes. This is followed by the immediate process of removing, straining, and plunging the food into a prepared ice bath to halt cooking.

Braise To start cooking a bigger piece of meat by searing it in little or no liquid or oil and finish cooking it in liquid in your oven. This method applies to pot roasts or briskets.

Broil To cook in the oven with a flame or an electric coil above the food to cook the top of the food at a higher heat. This technique is most commonly used to melt cheese on top of casseroles and lasagna or to brown meringue atop a pie, but you can also cook thin meats quickly and evenly and achieve a char (blackened edges) indoors on thinly sliced or thin vegetables like asparagus. You'll want to keep your eye on foods under the broiler—they can quickly burn.

Grill To cook proteins, vegetables, or fruits on grates over a fire, or using a grill pan with raised ridges.

Parboil To partially cook a vegetable or grain in boiling water before finishing the cooking process in the oven.

Stir-Fry To cook meat and/or vegetables in a small amount of oil at a very high temperature in a wok or large sauté pan, stirring or shaking the pan to keep the food moving while it cooks.

Sweat To cook vegetables like onions and garlic in butter or oil over lower heat until tender and translucent.

liquids into the pan.) This setting is also good for making simple syrups and fruit compotes.

Medium-high Great for searing meats (browning to lock in juices) before roasting as well as shallow frying. This is the heat level you'll probably use most often.

High Used for bringing liquids to a boil. You can sear red meat on high to help you achieve a great crust, but keep a close eye on your food to prevent burning, and reduce the temperature as needed.

KID CHEF TIPS
. . . .

Always add the oil to a hot pan and heat it up before adding the food. How will you know when it's hot enough? It's hot enough for vegetables when the oil begins to move to fully cover your pan and shimmers with small, wavy lines. You want the meat/seafood to sizzle as it hits the pan, so wait just until you see the first wisps of smoke coming from the oil. Work quickly and carefully. If you wait, the oil can begin to burn. (If you ever feel the pan is too hot, carefully move it off the heat for a minute or so to allow it to cool down.)

Using your oven is simple, however. Just set the oven temperature according to the recipe, and allow it to preheat and reach that temperature before you put your food in.

SAFE TEMPERATURES FOR FOODS

As a budding chef, you'll likely have the opportunity to work with meats. These come with their own set of rules. When it comes to storing proteins (meats, poultry, and seafood), keeping them cold enough decreases the chance for bacterial growth. The recommended temperature for all refrigerators is 40°F.

While refrigerated, perishable proteins should be wrapped securely to maintain quality and to prevent their juices from contaminating other food.

Cook or freeze fresh poultry, seafood, and ground meats within 2 days. Other beef (such as steaks or roasts), veal, lamb, or pork should be cooked or frozen within 3 to 5 days.

According to the United States Department of Agriculture (USDA), proteins kept at temperatures above 40°F for more than 2 hours should not be consumed.

When it comes time to cook your meats, poultry, or seafood, safe temperatures vary depending on the type of protein. Particularly when it comes to beef, in addition to safe cooking temperatures, you'll want to consider the level of doneness that you prefer.

SAFE INTERNAL COOKING TEMPERATURES

PROTEIN	SAFE INTERNAL TEMPERATURE
Beef, rare (cool red center)	125°F*
Beef, medium-rare (warm red center)	135°F*
Beef, medium (warm pink center)	145°F*
Beef, medium-well (slightly pink center)	150°F*
Beef, well-done (no pink)	160°F*
Ground beef	160°F
Pork, medium-rare	145°F plus a 3-minute rest
Pork, medium	150°F
Pork, well-done	160°F
Ground pork	160°F
Fish	140°F
Chicken	165°F
Turkey	165°F

*The USDA recommends that steaks and roasts be cooked to 145°F (medium) and then rested for at least 3 minutes. To ensure food safety, ground beef should be cooked to a minimum of 160°F (well done). Be sure to check with a meat thermometer, as color alone is not a foolproof indicator.

lemon-pepper pork chops

PREP TIME
10 minutes

COOK TIME
10 minutes

SERVES
4

**TOOLS/
EQUIPMENT**
Nonstick skillet or
cast-iron pan

Spatula

Whisk

Meat
thermometer

4 boneless pork chops

Salt

1 tablespoon lemon-pepper seasoning,
or more to taste

3 tablespoons butter, divided

1 tablespoon coarse Dijon mustard

1 tablespoon Worcestershire sauce

Season the chops.
Season the pork chops with salt, then dust both
sides with the lemon-pepper seasoning.

Cook the chops.
In a nonstick skillet over medium-high heat, melt
2 tablespoons of butter. Once the pan is hot, carefully add the pork chops (you should hear a sizzle
when they hit the pan). Cook, flipping once after
3 to 4 minutes. Cook for an additional 2 to 3 minutes on the second side. Cook time will depend on
the thickness of the chops. The chops should be
golden brown with crispy edges and register 160°F
on a meat thermometer for well done.

Make the sauce and coat.
Transfer the chops to a plate. Add the remaining
tablespoon of butter, mustard, and Worcestershire
to the pan. Whisk until combined. Return the chops
to the pan, and heat for 1 minute, flipping to coat
the chops in the sauce. Remove from the heat
and serve.

HELPFUL HINT If you enjoy extra sauce
on your meat, you can double the
butter, mustard, and Worcestershire sauce
ingredient quantities.

BAKING SKILLS

Being able to bake up a delicious treat for your family and friends is something that will earn you rave reviews. Baking is fun, and desserts are always memorable, but baking is a more precise science than cooking—even slight alterations can make a big difference in your end result. Let's take a look at some baking basics.

Cracking an Egg

Many baked goods include eggs, and it's no fun when a hard shell ends up in a bite of spongy cake. To ensure shell-free baked goods, always crack eggs against the counter and then empty into a small bowl. That way, if a piece of shell ends up in the egg, you can easily pick it out before you add it to your recipe. One more tip: Don't crack eggs against the bowl, or you'll probably end up with tiny pieces of shell in there.

Melting or Softening Butter

Many recipes call for melted, softened, or room-temperature butter; this makes it much easier to mix in. I like to leave my butter at room temperature because it's easy to work with. The USDA says butter can be kept at room temperature for two days or more, depending on how cool a house is. When a recipe calls for melted butter, use the microwave in 30-second bursts to melt the butter in a microwave-safe bowl covered with a paper towel. For room-temperature or softened butter, allow the butter to sit out at room temperature for a couple of hours prior to using.

KID CHEF TIPS

Make sure your baking soda is fresh (not more than three months old). Old baking soda can prevent baked goods from rising successfully, and that is such a disappointment!

Mixing Wet and Dry Ingredients

Typically, baking recipes will direct you to first mix together the dry ingredients in a bowl and set them aside, then mix the wet ingredients together in a separate bowl until blended and smooth. Finally, you'll add the dry ingredients to the wet ingredients and mix until the dough or batter is smooth. More often than not, you can use a mixer to do this.

When you make biscuits, fresh pasta, or breads, often the recipe will call for you to make a "well" or a hole (like the top of a volcano) in the center of your pile of dry ingredients, pour the wet ingredients into the hole, and then work on incorporating the wet and dry ingredients by hand.

Some recipes, like quick breads, allow for both wet and dry ingredients to be mixed all together. But since baking is more of a precise science than cooking, following the recipe instructions as closely as possible is best.

OVEN SAFETY

Always be careful when using your oven. Before you turn it on, move your oven racks to the position(s) recommended in the recipe (if no direction is given, the center rack is usually best for baking). When placing dishes into a hot oven, be careful not to touch the top or sides of the oven by accident. If your arms don't easily reach the racks, ask an adult to move your baked goods in and out of the oven for you.

Always use potholders to remove anything from the oven. If you removed a pan with a handle, remember not to accidentally grab the very hot handle. One trick: Slide an oven mitt onto the hot handle after removing it from the oven.

Always use two oven mitts, even if you think you only need one. Sometimes you'll find out a dish or pan is too heavy for one hand as you attempt to pull it out.

Be careful when you open an oven door; sometimes a burst of hot steam will escape. Also be careful of hot liquids as you pull out a dish from the oven so they don't splash you.

PREP TIME
10 minutes

COOK TIME
20 minutes

SERVES
6

TOOLS/ EQUIPMENT

Baking sheet

Parchment paper or silicone baking mat

2 large bowls

Mixer

Spatula

Ice cream scoop (optional)

3 cups old-fashioned oatmeal

1¼ cups all-purpose flour

½ teaspoon baking powder

¼ teaspoon baking soda

Dash salt

14 ounces (1¾ sticks) unsalted butter, very soft

2 tablespoons vegetable oil

1 cup sugar

1 cup brown sugar

2 large eggs

1½ teaspoons vanilla extract

1 cup raisins

¾ cup chocolate chips

 HELPFUL HINT You can either cook these in batches or use two baking sheets.

Preheat the oven.
Preheat the oven to 350°F. Line a baking sheet with parchment paper or a silicone baking mat.

Mix the dry ingredients.
In a large bowl, mix together the oatmeal, flour, baking powder, baking soda, and salt. Set aside.

Mix the remaining ingredients.
In another large bowl, combine the butter, oil, and both sugars, and blend until creamy. Stir in the eggs and vanilla until combined. Add the flour-oatmeal mixture, and blend until combined. Stir in the raisins and chocolate chips, mixing well to distribute.

Scoop big cookies.
Use an ice cream scoop to scoop out the cookie dough onto the lined baking sheet. If you don't have an ice cream scoop, measure about 3 table-spoons of dough per cookie; you want these very big. Place 6 to 8 scoops per baking sheet, depending on the size of the sheet, without crowding the cookies.

Bake the cookies.
Bake for 16 to 18 minutes, or until golden brown. Cool and serve.

TRY INSTEAD Customize these to your taste buds by substituting or adding in dried cranberries, nuts, shredded coconut, ground cinnamon or cardamom, or whatever flavors you enjoy most.

COOKING WITH FROZEN INGREDIENTS

Using previously frozen meats, poultry, and seafood is a common practice. Learn what you need to know to work safely and effectively with these foods.

Thawing Meats

The best way to thaw frozen meat is to plan it out a day or two ahead. Place the frozen meat, in its original packaging, on a baking sheet or plate, and allow it to thaw in your refrigerator for a day or two.

But we can't always plan ahead! If you're in a rush, take your wrapped meat and place it in a resealable freezer bag. Fill a large bowl with cold water and submerge the bag. Change the water every 30 minutes, until thawed. A 5-pound piece of meat could take 3 or more hours to thaw.

There are a few "nevers":

- Never allow meat to be at room temperature for more than 90 minutes.
- Never refreeze thawed meat.
- Try never to defrost meat in a microwave; that can ruin meat by partially cooking it.
- Never cook partially frozen meat. It will not cook evenly, and parts of it may come out unsafe to eat.

That said, there's one "always": Always allow thawed meat to sit at room temperature 30 minutes prior to cooking it—this allows for even cooking.

> ### KID CHEF TIPS
>
> Freeze your own delicious summer strawberries. They are great for use later in smoothies and baked goods.

Brown bananas might not look yummy, but they can be peeled frozen and made into the most delicious smoothies and even banana bread.

Frozen Veggies

Did you know that typically, frozen fruits and vegetables from markets have been frozen just after they were harvested, making them fresher than much of the produce you see in the grocery store? They are literally as fresh as the day they were harvested! Many families who either garden or belong to a community-supported agriculture group (CSA) freeze their own. Some people buy up boatloads of vegetables at their peak from farmers' markets or supermarkets and freeze them for later use. Choosing to use frozen fruits and vegetables comes down to personal preference. Most recipes can work with either fresh or frozen.

FROZEN DOUGH AND PIECRUSTS

Piecrusts and doughs can be made at home or bought either fresh or frozen. It's great to have frozen on hand for the moment you suddenly decide to make something. You also save on preparation time and cleanup. Experiment with making your own, buying fresh, and buying frozen to see which you prefer. I prefer to make my own so that I can say I truly "made" the dessert.

LESSON 5 RECIPE TUTORIAL
skillet veggie & beef mac & cheese

PREP TIME
10 minutes

COOK TIME
30 minutes

SERVES
4

TOOLS/ EQUIPMENT

Large skillet

Spatula

Small plastic measuring cup, spoon, or baster

1 pound frozen ground beef, thawed

1 teaspoon salt

½ teaspoon freshly ground black pepper

1 (14.5-ounce) bag frozen stir-fry vegetable mix, thawed

8 ounces uncooked elbow macaroni

2 cups marinara sauce

2 cups water

⅓ cup half-and-half

½ cup shredded mozzarella cheese

Pinch red pepper flakes (optional)

Brown the beef.

In a large skillet over medium heat, cook the ground beef, breaking it apart with a spatula and sprinkling with the salt and pepper, until the meat is browned, 7 to 10 minutes. Use a small spoon or baster to drain off the fat, keeping the beef in the skillet.

Cook the veggies and pasta.

Add the stir-fry vegetables, macaroni, marinara sauce, and water. Bring to a boil, then reduce the heat to a simmer. Simmer, covered but stirring occasionally, for about 20 minutes, until the macaroni is tender.

Melt the cheese and serve.

Add the half-and-half, sprinkle with the cheese and red pepper flakes (if using), and mix well. Remove from the heat. Cover and let it sit for 2 to 3 minutes, or until the cheese melts, and serve.

 TRY INSTEAD Swap out the ground beef for ground turkey, chicken, or pork.

Recipes

I'm SO excited for you to cook through the recipes in this book! I hope some will become your family favorites and that maybe a few become your signature dishes—the recipes you become famous for in your circle of family and friends. Happy cooking!

Honey-Lime Fruit Salad (page 60)

breakfast

43

mango-banana smoothie

PREP TIME
5 minutes

SERVES
2

**TOOLS/
EQUIPMENT**
Blender

2 cups frozen mango chunks

½ banana

¾ cup whole milk

1 teaspoon honey

1 cup ice

Blend and enjoy.

In a blender, combine all the ingredients. Blend until smooth. Pour into 2 glasses and enjoy.

DID YOU KNOW? More mango is eaten around the world each day than any other fruit.

homemade breakfast sausage

PREP TIME
10 minutes,
plus 15 minutes
to chill

COOK TIME
6 minutes

SERVES

6

**TOOLS/
EQUIPMENT**
Cutting board
Knife
Large bowl
Large nonstick
frying pan or
sauté pan
Plastic or
silicone spatula

2 pounds ground pork

1 tablespoon maple syrup

1½ teaspoons kosher salt

1 teaspoon freshly ground
black pepper

⅛ teaspoon red pepper flakes

2 garlic cloves, minced,
or 2 tablespoons garlic paste

1 tablespoon chopped fresh sage

1 teaspoon chopped fresh thyme

1 tablespoon olive oil or grapeseed oil

TRY INSTEAD Try this
recipe with ground
chicken or turkey instead
of pork.

Form the patties.
In a large bowl, combine all the ingredients except
the oil. Mix with your hands until fully blended.
Cover and refrigerate for 15 to 30 minutes. Form
into patties.

Brown the sausage and serve.
In a large nonstick pan over medium-high heat, heat
the oil (use more if needed). Cook the patties, allowing a little room between them, for 2½ to 3 minutes
per side, or until browned and cooked through,
and serve.

NOTE You can cut this recipe in half for
a smaller batch, or you can freeze
uncooked or cooked patties by placing them
on a parchment- or wax paper–lined baking
sheet and freezing them for 2 hours. Transfer
frozen patties into a freezer-safe bag and
freeze for up to 3 months. Mark the date
you freeze them on the bag with perma-
nent marker.

PRO TIP You can use dried herbs instead
of fresh, although the taste won't be
quite as fresh or vibrant. Use one-third as
much dried as you would fresh (1 tablespoon
of fresh herbs equals 1 teaspoon of dried).

huevos mexicanos (mexican scrambled eggs)

PREP TIME
10 minutes

COOK TIME
10 minutes

SERVES
4

**TOOLS/
EQUIPMENT**
Cutting board
Knife
1 medium bowl
and 1 small bowl
Whisk
Small spoon
Large sauté pan
Spatula

8 large eggs

1 jalapeño pepper, or less if desired

¼ cup minced onion

1 small tomato

1 tablespoon olive oil

Salt

Freshly ground black pepper

TRY INSTEAD You can add ¼ to ½ cup of shredded cheese and/or ½ cup of crumbled chorizo. You can also wrap this up in a tortilla to create a breakfast burrito.

Whisk the eggs.
Crack the eggs into a medium bowl. Whisk them until frothy, and set aside.

Chop the jalapeño.
Decide whether to use the whole jalapeño or half, depending on how spicy you like it. Cut the sides of the jalapeño, leaving the stem and seeds to throw away. Scrape off any remaining seeds. Chop the jalapeño, and scrape into a small bowl with the onion.

Dice the tomato.
Core the tomato by cutting around the tomato core. Discard the core. Scrape out the seeds and juicy pulp with a small spoon. Dice the tomato and add to the bowl with the jalapeño.

Cook the ingredients and serve.
In a large sauté pan over medium-high heat, heat the oil. Add the jalapeño, tomato, and onion and cook, stirring occasionally, until tender, about 5 minutes. Turn the heat down to low, add the eggs, and cook, folding the eggs over occasionally with a spatula. Season with salt and pepper. Cook for about 4 minutes, or until done to your liking, and serve.

TROUBLESHOOTING Be especially careful when working with the seeds and stems of the jalapeños. If you have gloves, wear them when cutting them. Otherwise, the oil from the jalapeños will stay on your fingers for hours, even if you wash them well, so avoid touching your face.

egg & cheese breakfast loaf

PREP TIME
10 minutes

COOK TIME
20 minutes

SERVES
4 TO 6

TOOLS/ EQUIPMENT
Cutting board
Knife
Baking sheet

1 loaf ciabatta bread or French bread

4 to 6 large eggs

2 to 3 tablespoons heavy or light cream, divided

1 tablespoon chopped fresh parsley

1 tablespoon chopped scallion

Salt

Freshly ground black pepper

2 to 3 tablespoons shredded Parmesan or Cheddar cheese

Preheat the oven.
Preheat the oven to 350°F.

Assemble the loaf.
Set the bread on a baking sheet. Depending on the size of your bread loaf, cut 4 to 6 circles in the top ½ inch or so apart and about 2 inches in diameter. Scoop out the bread from the circles about an inch deep to form holes.

Fill the holes.
Crack an egg into each hole, top each with ½ table- spoon of cream and some parsley, scallions, salt, and pepper. Sprinkle with the cheese.

Bake and serve.
Bake for 20 minutes, or until the eggs are done to your liking. Cut into equal size pieces and serve.

TRY INSTEAD Spoon a little crumbled cooked sausage into each hole in the bread loaf before adding the eggs. Or top with crispy crumbled bacon just before serving. You can add sautéed spinach on top as well, or you can nestle the bread onto a plate of spinach. You can also make these in individual crusty rolls. The options are almost endless.

broccoli & cheese quiche

PREP TIME
10 minutes

COOK TIME
50 minutes, plus
10 minutes to set

SERVES
6

**TOOLS/
EQUIPMENT**

Grater

Deep-dish pie pan
(if needed)

Rimmed
baking sheet

Large bowl

Whisk

Mixing spoon

Knife

1 frozen deep-dish piecrust

1½ cups whole milk

3 large eggs

1 tablespoon flour

1 tablespoon melted butter

Dash salt

Dash freshly ground black pepper

½ cup diced broccoli (frozen and
thawed works best)

6 ounces shredded Cheddar cheese

Preheat the oven.
Preheat the oven to 375°F.

Prepare the crust.
If your pie dough is not already in a disposable
pie tin, press it into a deep-dish pie pan. Place the
dough-filled pie pan on a rimmed baking sheet.

Mix the ingredients.
In a large bowl, whisk together the milk, eggs, flour,
butter, salt, and pepper until combined. Stir in the
broccoli and cheese.

Pour, bake, and serve.
Pour the mixture into the pie pan, being careful not
to overfill past three-quarters full. Place the pie on
the rimmed baking sheet in the oven, and bake for
45 to 50 minutes, or until the quiche is puffed up
and golden brown on top. Once removed from the
oven, allow the quiche to set for at least 10 minutes
before slicing and serving.

TRY INSTEAD For extra flavor and color,
add 1 cup of diced ham or some
crumbled bacon in addition to, or in place of,
the broccoli.

country breakfast potatoes

PREP TIME
10 minutes

COOK TIME
20 minutes

SERVES
6

**TOOLS/
EQUIPMENT**

Cutting board

Paring or
chef's knife

Microwave-
safe dish

Kitchen shears
(optional)

Large skillet

Slotted spoon

Spatula

Paper towel

Plate

4 russet potatoes (or your favorite
potato variety)

½ pound bacon

1 large red or green pepper, diced

1 medium sweet onion, diced

Freshly ground black pepper

Pinch salt

HELPFUL HINT You do
not have to start
cooking the potatoes in the
microwave; however, that
trick cuts the cooking time in
half and doesn't overcook
the potatoes.

Prep the potatoes.

Scrub the potatoes, removing dirt and debris. Cut
the potatoes into even, bite-size chunks. Place in a
microwave-safe dish, partially covered, and microwave for 3 minutes. Allow the potatoes to cool.

Cook the bacon.

Meanwhile, using kitchen shears or a knife, cut
the bacon into 1-inch pieces. In a large skillet over
medium heat, carefully sauté on both sides until
just crisp, about 8 minutes. Using a slotted spoon or
spatula, transfer the bacon to a paper towel–lined
plate, reserving the bacon fat in the pan.

Cook the veggies and serve.

Add the peppers and onion to the pan with the
hot bacon fat. Cook over medium heat, stirring
occasionally, for 3 minutes, or until the peppers are
tender. Add the potatoes, season well with pepper
and a pinch of salt (the bacon drippings are already
salty), and continue cooking until the potatoes crisp
up a bit, about 4 minutes. Add the crispy bacon
pieces, toss, and serve.

TROUBLESHOOTING If you don't want to
add bacon, use olive or grapeseed oil to
keep the food from sticking to the pan.

FOOD FACT Potatoes are an awesome
source of vitamins B6 and C, potassium,
and fiber—especially with the skin on. They
contain more potassium than bananas!

buttermilk pancakes with berry compote

PREP TIME
10 minutes, plus
10 minutes to sit

COOK TIME
3 to 4 minutes
per batch

SERVES

**TOOLS/
EQUIPMENT**
Cutting board
Knife
1 medium bowl
and 1 small bowl
Whisk
Large,
nonstick skillet
Ice cream
scoop or ⅓ cup
measuring cup
Spatula
Small pot
Small mesh
strainer

FOR THE PANCAKES
1½ cups flour

2 tablespoons sugar

2 teaspoons baking powder

½ teaspoon baking soda

Pinch salt

1 large egg

1½ cups buttermilk

1½ tablespoons melted butter

1 pint blueberries

FOR THE COMPOTE
1 pint strawberries,
hulled and quartered

¼ cup granulated sugar

3 tablespoons water

½ tablespoon fresh squeezed
lemon juice

Powdered sugar, for sprinkling

Mix the dry ingredients.
In a medium bowl, combine the flour, sugar, baking powder, baking soda, and salt, and whisk until all ingredients are incorporated. Set aside.

Mix the wet ingredients.
In a small bowl, whisk the egg. Add the buttermilk and butter, and whisk until combined.

Mix the wet and dry ingredients together.
Add the wet ingredients to the dry ingredients, and whisk just until combined. Do not overmix; some lumps are okay. Allow the batter to sit for about 10 minutes.

Make the compote.
While the batter sits, in a small pot over medium-high heat, combine all the compote ingredients, except the powdered sugar. Bring to a simmer. After 2 minutes, remove the pot from the heat and allow to cool down. The compote can be made a day ahead and stored in a mason jar or lidded container.

Cook the pancakes.
When ready to cook, set a large, nonstick skillet over medium-high heat. Use an ice cream scoop or a ⅓ cup measuring cup to scoop the batter and pour it into the pan, making "puddles" of batter. Quickly arrange the blueberries on top. Once bubbles form and pop, flip the pancakes and cook through.

Assemble and serve.

Use a small mesh strainer to top the pancakes with a nice sprinkle of powdered sugar; add a couple spoonfuls of the berry compote and serve.

TRY INSTEAD Instead of putting blueberries in the batter, make a quick compote. All you need is 4 cups of blueberries (fresh is best, but frozen works, too), ⅓ cup of water, ⅓ cup of sugar, a pinch of ground cinnamon, a pinch of ground cardamom (optional), and ¾ teaspoon of cornstarch. In a small pot, combine the blueberries, water, and sugar. Heat over medium-high heat until the berries start to release their juice and burst, about 5 minutes, stirring occasionally. Lower the heat to medium. Add the spices and cornstarch, and stir until thickened, about 2 minutes. Remove from the heat and allow to cool. Spoon the compote over the pancakes and enjoy. This compote is great over cheesecake and ice cream, too.

breakfast pizza

PREP TIME
15 minutes

COOK TIME
15 minutes

SERVES

4

**TOOLS/
EQUIPMENT**

Grater

4 small bowls
or ramekins

Pizza stone or
baking sheet

Basting brush
(or paper towel)

Large bowl

Pizza cutter
or knife

Flour, for dusting the pan

1 disk fresh pizza dough, store-bought
or from a pizza shop

Olive oil

Salt

Freshly ground black pepper

15 asparagus spears, woody
ends trimmed

10 slices Virginia ham, torn into pieces

1 cup shredded Monterey Jack cheese

½ cup shredded mozzarella

4 large eggs, each cracked into a
separate small bowl or ramekin

Prepare the oven.
Position an oven rack in the middle of the oven. Prepare a pizza stone or baking sheet by scattering flour lightly onto the surface. Preheat the oven to 450°F.

Prepare the dough.
Shape the pizza dough into either a rustic rectangle or a traditional round, depending on the shape of your pan. Brush the dough lightly with oil, and season with salt and pepper.

Add the asparagus.
Place a small amount of oil in your clean hands. In a large bowl, toss the asparagus spears with your hands, lightly coating them. Season the asparagus with salt and pepper, then arrange the asparagus in a sunburst pattern, with the tips pointing outward.

Bake the pizza and eggs and serve.
Place in the oven and bake for 5 minutes. Remove from the oven, place ham all over the pizza, top with the cheeses, and slide each egg onto a separate quarter of the pizza. Sprinkle the eggs with salt and pepper, and quickly return the pizza to the oven. Bake for an additional 10 minutes, or until the crust is golden and the eggs are set to your liking. Cool slightly, slice into 4 wedges, and serve.

TRY INSTEAD You can add crumbled cooked sausage, bacon, or prosciutto instead of the ham, or make this a veggie pizza with raw baby spinach, grape tomato halves, or whatever veggies you enjoy.

TROUBLESHOOTING If you don't want to place raw eggs directly onto the pizza, while the pizza bakes, fry the eggs one at a time in a small, lightly oiled skillet over medium-high heat. Do not flip. Season the eggs with salt and pepper and place onto the pizza. Return the pizza to the oven until the eggs are set to your liking.

fruit & granola parfait

PREP TIME
10 minutes

SERVES
4

**TOOLS/
EQUIPMENT**

Cutting board
(if needed)

Knife (if needed)

4 large glass jars,
mugs, or stemless
wine glasses

24 ounces vanilla Greek yogurt

2 cups granola

2 tablespoons honey

2 cups of your favorite fruits, such as
berries or chopped pineapple, kiwi,
peaches, etc.

Layer the ingredients and serve.
Into each of 4 glasses, spoon a layer of yogurt, then
a layer of granola. Drizzle the granola layer with a little honey. Top that layer with a layer of fruit. Repeat.
Top with another drizzle of honey and enjoy.

TRY INSTEAD Instead of using glassware
for your parfait, purchase a pineapple,
halve it right down the middle, top to bottom,
carefully cut out most of the fruit from the
skin, and then cut the fruit into chunks,
discarding the bitter center core. Use the
remaining pineapple "boats" to create the
parfaits. Then dig in! Eat this pretty, festive
treat while envisioning yourself on a
tropical island.

banana coffee cake

PREP TIME
10 minutes

COOK TIME
50 minutes

SERVES
6

**TOOLS/
EQUIPMENT**

Cutting board

Knife

13-by-9-inch
baking dish

1 small,
1 large, and
1 medium bowl

Whisk

Potato masher

Pastry cutter
(optional)

Toothpick

FOR THE CAKE
Nonstick cooking spray

2 cups all-purpose flour

2½ tablespoons baking powder

½ teaspoon salt

3 overripe bananas

2 cups granulated sugar

1 cup whole milk

½ cup melted and cooled butter

2 large eggs

1 teaspoon vanilla extract

FOR THE CRUMB TOPPING
1½ cups brown sugar

1½ cups all-purpose flour

6 tablespoons cold butter, cut into
12 pieces

Preheat the oven.
Preheat the oven to 350°F. Spray a 13-by-9-inch baking dish with cooking spray. Set aside.

Mix the dry ingredients.
In a small bowl, whisk together the flour, baking powder, and salt. Set aside.

Mix the batter.
In a large bowl, mash the bananas with a potato masher until mushy. Add the granulated sugar, milk, butter, eggs, and vanilla, and stir until fully combined. Add the flour mixture, and mix until fully combined. Scrape the batter into the prepared baking dish.

Add the topping.
In a medium bowl, combine the brown sugar, flour, and butter. Using a pastry cutter or your fingertips, blend until the mixture resembles crumbs. Sprinkle the topping over the batter.

Bake the cake and serve.
Bake for 45 to 50 minutes, or until a toothpick inserted into the middle comes out dry. Allow the cake to cool, then cut into squares and serve.

 ADD-INS If you like nuts, add ½ cup of chopped pecans or walnuts to the topping.

blueberry scones

PREP TIME
10 minutes

COOK TIME
20 minutes

SERVES
6

**TOOLS/
EQUIPMENT**

Cutting board

Knife

Microplane
or zester

Baking sheet

Parchment
paper or silicone
baking mat

Large bowl

Whisk

Mixing spoon

Pastry cutter
(optional)

Chef's knife

Pastry brush

Toothpick

1½ cups all-purpose flour, plus more
for scattering

¼ cup sugar, plus more for sprinkling

½ tablespoon baking powder

⅛ teaspoon salt

6 tablespoons cold butter,
cut into 12 pieces

½ cup dried blueberries
(see Helpful Hint)

½ cup buttermilk, plus more for
brushing the dough

½ tablespoon lemon zest

Preheat the oven.
Preheat the oven to 400°F. Line a baking sheet with parchment paper or a silicone baking mat

Mix the ingredients.
In a large bowl, combine the flour, sugar, baking powder, and salt, and whisk together. Using a pastry cutter or your clean fingertips, work the butter into the flour mixture until it resembles pea-size balls. Add the blueberries, stirring to combine. Add the buttermilk and lemon peel, and mix until a dough forms.

Prepare the dough.
Scatter some flour onto a clean countertop. Transfer the dough to the floured counter, and use your hands to work it until all the flour is mixed in. Shape the dough into a round disk. Break the dough into two pieces and shape into two 1-inch-high disks. Transfer the disks to the prepared baking sheet. Using a chef's knife, cut each disk into 4 to 6 wedges. Space the wedges slightly apart.

Bake the scones and serve.
Brush the tops of the dough with a bit of buttermilk, and sprinkle with sugar and lemon zest. Bake for 15 to 20 minutes, or until a toothpick inserted into the thickest part comes out mostly clean, and serve.

 HELPFUL HINT Dried blueberries are better for this recipe than fresh, since fresh have a high water content and may make the scones mushy.

pumpkin donut muffins

PREP TIME
10 minutes

COOK TIME
10 minutes

SERVES
6

**TOOLS/
EQUIPMENT**

Mini muffin pan

1 medium bowl,
1 large bowl, and
2 small bowls

Mixing spoon

Toothpick

Parchment paper

Wire rack
(optional)

FOR THE MUFFINS
Nonstick cooking spray

1¾ cups flour

1½ teaspoons baking powder

1½ teaspoons pumpkin pie spice

¼ to ½ cup butter, melted

½ teaspoon salt

1 cup pumpkin purée
(not pumpkin pie filling)

¾ cup sugar

⅓ cup vegetable oil

1 large egg

FOR THE COATING
⅓ cup sugar

1 tablespoon pumpkin pie spice

¼ to ½ cup butter, melted

 TRY INSTEAD These can
be cooked in regular
muffin pans, too. Just
increase the cook time to
22 to 25 minutes.

Preheat the oven.
Preheat the oven to 350°F, and spray a mini muffin pan with cooking spray.

Mix the dry ingredients.
In a medium bowl, mix together the flour, baking powder, pumpkin pie spice, and salt. Set aside.

Mix the wet ingredients.
In a large bowl, combine the pumpkin purée, sugar, oil, and egg. Add the dry ingredients to the wet ingredients, and stir until combined.

Bake the muffins.
Fill the muffin cups three-quarters full with batter. Bake for 8 to 9 minutes, or until a toothpick inserted into the center of a muffin comes out clean.

Prepare the coating.
In a small bowl, mix the sugar and pumpkin pie spice. Set this bowl next to your bowl of melted butter.

Coat and serve.
Transfer the muffins onto parchment paper. While still hot, dip them one by one into the melted butter, then immediately roll in the sugar mixture, coating the muffin entirely. Enjoy hot or place on a wire rack to cool.

PRO TIP Make your own pumpkin pie spice by combining ¼ cup of ground cinnamon, 3 teaspoons of ground ginger, 3 teaspoons of ground nutmeg, 1 teaspoon of ground allspice, and 1 teaspoon of ground cloves. Whisk well and store in an airtight container until ready to use.

cinnamon bun baked oatmeal

PREP TIME
10 minutes

COOK TIME
30 minutes, plus
5 minutes to sit

SERVES
6

**TOOLS/
EQUIPMENT**
Cutting board
Knife
Peeler
8-by-8-inch
baking dish
Large bowl
Mixing spoon

Nonstick cooking spray

2 cups old-fashioned oats

2 teaspoons ground cinnamon
or apple pie spice

Pinch salt

1 heaping cup peeled, diced
Granny Smith apples

¾ cup Cinnamon Applesauce (page 64)
or apple butter

¼ cup whole milk

¼ cup grapeseed or olive oil

2 large eggs

3 tablespoons maple syrup,
plus more for drizzling

Preheat the oven.
Preheat the oven to 350°F. Spray an 8-by-8-inch
baking dish with cooking spray, and set aside.

Mix the ingredients.
In a large bowl, combine all the ingredients and stir
until fully blended.

Bake the oatmeal and serve.
Scrape the batter into the prepared baking dish
and spread evenly. Bake for 30 minutes, or until
golden brown on top. Allow to sit for 5 minutes
before serving. Drizzle with additional maple syrup
if desired, and enjoy!

TRY INSTEAD This dish can be baked in
individual oven-safe ramekins or bowls
sprayed with cooking spray; just reduce the
baking time to 15 minutes. You can also add in
¼ cup or more of chopped pecans or walnuts
for a nutty crunch.

honey-lime fruit salad

PREP TIME:
15 minutes

SERVES
4

TOOLS/
EQUIPMENT

Cutting board

Knife

Microplane
or zester

Serving bowl

1 cup strawberries, halved

1 cup blueberries

1 cup grapes, halved

Zest of ½ lime

2 tablespoons freshly
squeezed lime juice

2 tablespoons honey (more to taste
if you want it sweeter)

Mix the fruit.

In a serving bowl, toss together the strawberries, blueberries, and grapes.

Flavor and serve.

Sprinkle the lime zest onto the fruit, toss with the lime juice, and serve.

 ADD-INS Banana chunks are another delicious addition.

HELPFUL HINT If your strawberries are not very sweet, try macerating them for 5 to 10 minutes. Macerating is a fancy term for adding sugar to fruit to soften and sweeten it. To do this, simply add ½ tablespoon of sugar.

Avocado Dip (page 73)

snacks & small bites

cinnamon applesauce

PREP TIME
10 minutes

COOK TIME
25 minutes

SERVES
6

**TOOLS/
EQUIPMENT**
Peeler
Cutting board
Knife
Medium pot
Mixing spoon
Potato masher
(or fork)

8 apples (4 each of 2 varieties, such as Golden Delicious, Pink Lady, Fuji, Gala, or Granny Smith), peeled, cored, and cut into 1-inch pieces

1½ cups water

3 tablespoons brown sugar

2 cinnamon sticks or 1 teaspoon ground cinnamon

Cook the apples.
In a medium pot, mix together all the ingredients. Cover and cook over medium heat for 20 to 25 minutes, or until the apples are cooked through (see Helpful Hints). Remove the mixture from the heat and allow to cool down for a few minutes.

Mash the apples.
With a potato masher or the back of a fork, mash the apples. Once mashed to your liking, allow to cool in the pot. Once cool, spoon the applesauce into a container or jars and refrigerate for up to a week.

 HELPFUL HINTS To tell if the apples are cooked enough, remove an apple chunk, cool it down, and see if you can easily smush it between your finger and thumb. Apple varieties vary in sweetness. Depending on which you choose, you may not need to add any sugar. This applesauce is delicious by itself or stirred into oatmeal.

6-minute salsa

PREP TIME
6 minutes

SERVES
6+

**TOOLS/
EQUIPMENT**

Food processor
or high-powered
blender

FOR THE SALSA

1 jalapeño (see Helpful Hints)

3 large garlic cloves

1 (28-ounce) can fire-roasted tomatoes

2 tablespoons freshly squeezed
lime juice

2 tablespoons honey

¼ teaspoon ground cumin

Dash kosher salt

Dash freshly ground black pepper

FOR SERVING

Tortilla chips

Blend and serve.

In a food processor or high-powered blender, combine the jalapeño and garlic. Pulse or blend until minced, add in the remaining salsa ingredients, and pulse or blend until smooth. Taste and adjust for sweetness and heat. Serve with tortilla chips.

HELPFUL HINTS If you enjoy some heat in your salsa, include some or all of the seeds and stems from the jalapeño. However, taste a small piece of the jalapeño first—it is very hot! If you like it milder, only use half. If the jalapeño is not very spicy, you can add in a few pinches of ground cayenne pepper. To make this salsa sweeter, add more honey. This is a delicious and flexible recipe that you can make your own.

strawberry-lime refrigerator jam

PREP TIME
10 minutes

COOK TIME
15 minutes

MAKES

12
OUNCES

**TOOLS/
EQUIPMENT**

Cutting board

Knife

Microplane
or zester

Medium pot

Potato masher or
wooden spoon

Heat-safe spoon
or spatula

Mason jar or glass
bowl with lid

2 pounds fresh strawberries,
washed and hulled, diced small

¼ cup freshly squeezed lime juice

1½ cups sugar

1 tablespoon lime zest

Pinch kosher salt

Mash the strawberries.

In a medium pot, combine all the ingredients.
Mash the mixture with a potato masher.

Cook the jam.

Bring the mixture to a boil, stirring occasionally.
Reduce the heat to medium-low and simmer for
15 minutes, stirring often. The mixture will foam up,
but as it cooks down, it will calm down and thicken a
little. Test for doneness by dipping a spoon or spatula in every so often. When it drips off the spoon in
sections, remove from the heat.

Cool and store.

Allow the mixture to cool completely. Refrigerate
in a mason jar or covered glass bowl with a lid for up
to 2 weeks.

TROUBLESHOOTING Use a larger pot than
you need to prevent the jam from
splattering. If the jam is not as thick as you
would like once it has completely chilled, you
can return it to the pot and allow it to boil
again for 7 to 10 minutes. Repeat the cooling
process. It may take a couple of tries making
this until you can tell when the jam reaches
the right consistency.

grape salsa

TOOLS/ EQUIPMENT

Cutting board

Knife

Small bowl

Small jar with lid

2 cups red and green grapes, quartered

2 tablespoons minced red onion

1 tablespoon minced fresh cilantro

2 tablespoons freshly squeezed lime juice

1 tablespoon honey

½ teaspoon red wine vinegar

Pita chips or tortilla chips, for serving

Make the salsa.
In a small bowl, combine the grapes, onion, and cilantro, and toss to mix.

Combine the liquid ingredients and serve.
In a small jar with a lid, combine the lime juice, honey, and vinegar, and shake until it emulsifies. Pour the liquid over the salsa, and toss to coat. Serve with pita chips or tortilla chips.

DID YOU KNOW? You can make this salsa as spicy or as sweet as you like. It would also be delicious over a simple pan-sautéed or oven-roasted flakey white fish or salmon.

quick pickles

PREP TIME
15 minutes

COOK TIME
5 minutes

MAKES
3
QUART JARS

**TOOLS/
EQUIPMENT**
Cutting board
Knife
Large bowl
Tongs or 2 forks
3 quart-size
mason jars
Small pot

4 or 5 large cucumbers, sliced thin

2 large red onions, sliced thin

3 cups white vinegar

1¾ cups sugar

1½ tablespoons kosher salt

1 tablespoon celery flakes

1 to 2 teaspoons red pepper flakes
(depending how spicy you like it)

3 cups ice

Prepare the veggies.
In a large bowl, toss the sliced cucumbers and onions using tongs or 2 forks. Fill each jar with the vegetable mixture, using a spoon to gently push the veggies down to make room for more.

Cook the pickle juice.
In a small pot, combine the vinegar, sugar, salt, celery flakes, and red pepper flakes, to taste. Bring to a boil. Remove the pot from the heat, and add the ice. Stir until the ice is melted. Fill the jars with the mixture just below the top.

Cool and store.
Cover and allow the jars to cool to room temperature, then refrigerate until ready to enjoy.

TRY INSTEAD If onions are not your thing, feel free to leave them out and substitute an extra cucumber.

DID YOU KNOW? It is believed the first pickle was created in Mesopotamia in 2400 BC.

onion soufflé dip

PREP TIME
5 minutes

COOK TIME
30 minutes

SERVES
6

**TOOLS/
EQUIPMENT**
Cutting board
Knife
Grater (if needed)
Large bowl
Spatula
Small baking dish

FOR THE DIP
1 (8-ounce) block cream cheese at room temperature or softened

1 cup mayonnaise

1 cup shredded Parmesan cheese

1 cup diced Vidalia (sweet) onion

1 teaspoon freshly ground
black pepper

FOR SERVING
Flat pretzels, slices of French bread, or stone-ground wheat crackers

Preheat the oven.
Preheat the oven to 350°F.

Mix the ingredients.
In a large bowl, combine all the dip ingredients. Mix with a spatula until smooth, and scrape into a small baking dish. Let the mixture rest for a few minutes so the flavors mingle.

Bake and serve.
Bake for about 30 minutes, or until the top is brown in spots. Serve with flat pretzels, slices of French bread, or stoned wheat or stone-ground wheat crackers.

 HELPFUL HINTS Don't use low-fat cheese or mayo for this—only regular will do. Keep an eye out—the cheese can separate and become oily when cooked at too high a temperature or for too long.

veggie cream cheese spread

PREP TIME
10 minutes,
plus 30 minutes
to chill

SERVES

4 TO **6**

**TOOLS/
EQUIPMENT**

Cutting board

Knife

Small bowl

Spatula

Plastic wrap

1 (8-ounce) block cream cheese at room temperature

3 tablespoons minced carrot

3 tablespoons minced celery

3 tablespoons minced red bell pepper

2 scallions, snipped or sliced

NOTE This recipe is delicious as a spread for bagels or crackers, or as a dip for raw veggies or pretzels.

Mix the ingredients.

In a small bowl, combine all the ingredients. Using a spatula, mix until everything is blended and the cream cheese is smooth.

Cover and chill.

Cover with plastic wrap and refrigerate for at least 30 minutes to allow the flavors to blend, or until ready to serve.

 ADD-INS If you enjoy onion, add 1 table-spoon of minced red onion.

HELPFUL HINT If you have a food processor, cut the vegetables into 1-inch chunks and add to the processor; pulse until just minced. Add the cream cheese and pulse until just combined. Scrape into a ramekin or small bowl, cover, and refrigerate until ready to use.

avocado dip

PREP TIME
10 minutes,
plus 20 minutes
to chill

SERVES
6

**TOOLS/
EQUIPMENT**
Knife
Food processor or
high-powered
blender
Spatula
Serving bowl
Plastic wrap

FOR THE DIP
2 ripe avocados, peeled and pitted

6 ounces plain Greek yogurt

6 ounces sour cream

2 tablespoons garlic paste or 2 garlic
cloves, minced

2 tablespoons fresh cilantro leaves

1 tablespoon freshly squeezed
lime juice

2 dashes ground cumin

Dash kosher salt

Dash freshly ground black pepper

FOR SERVING
Tortilla chips, pita chips, or veggies

Blend the dip.
In a food processor or high-powered blender,
combine all the dip ingredients. Pulse until almost
smooth. Adjust the seasoning to your liking, then
scrape the dip into a serving bowl.

Wrap, chill, and serve.
Cover tightly with plastic wrap touching the dip
(to prevent browning), and chill for 20 to 30 minutes.
Serve with tortilla chips, pita chips, or veggies for
dipping.

> FOOD FACT Avocados were originally
> named "alligator pears." You can see
> why when you look at their skin.

edamame hummus

PREP TIME
10 minutes

COOK TIME
5 minutes

SERVES
6

**TOOLS/
EQUIPMENT**
Small pot
Colander or
strainer
Food processor
Rubber or
silicone spatula
Serving bowl

FOR THE HUMMUS
1½ cups shelled edamame

2 garlic cloves or 1 tablespoon
garlic paste

⅓ cup sesame oil (tahini)

¼ cup packed cilantro leaves

½ cup water

¼ cup freshly squeezed lemon juice

¼ cup olive oil

½ teaspoon ground cumin

½ teaspoon kosher salt

FOR SERVING
Pita chips, carrots, and celery

Cook the edamame.
In a small pot of salted water, boil the edamame until tender, 5 to 6 minutes. Drain in a colander, and rinse with cold water to cool. Set aside.

Blend and serve.
In a food processor, pulse the garlic until minced. Add the edamame and the remaining hummus ingredients, and process until smooth. Use a rubber or silicone spatula to transfer to a serving bowl, and serve with pita chips, carrots, and celery.

 PRO TIP Up your presentation game by saving a small handful of edamame to decorate the top of your bowl, and/or sprinkle with some chopped scallions and a dash of ground cumin. Drizzle a small amount of olive oil on top as well.

cheddar puffs

PREP TIME
10 minutes

COOK TIME
25 minutes

SERVES
4

**TOOLS/
EQUIPMENT**

Grater

Baking sheet

Parchment paper

Medium saucepan

Wooden spoon or
rubber spatula

Medium bowl

½ cup water

4 tablespoons butter

Pinch salt

½ cup all-purpose flour

Pinch freshly ground black pepper

1 large egg, plus 1 large egg white

½ cup grated extra-sharp
Cheddar cheese

Preheat the oven.
Preheat the oven to 400°F, and line a baking sheet
with parchment paper.

Melt the butter.
In a medium saucepan, bring the water, butter,
and salt to a simmer. When the butter has melted,
remove the pan from the heat. Add the flour and
pepper. Mix vigorously with a wooden spoon or
rubber spatula until it forms a thick dough.

Add the eggs and cheese.
Transfer the dough to a medium bowl. Using the
spoon or a mixer, add the egg and then the egg
white, continuing to mix until fully incorporated.
Allow the dough to cool to just slightly warm, then
mix in the cheese.

Bake the puffs.
Spoon 1-inch pieces of dough onto the baking
sheet about 1 inch apart. Bake until golden and
crisp, about 25 minutes. Serve warm.

TRY INSTEAD If desired, mix in a little
chopped scallion with the Cheddar
cheese. Like spicy food? Mix ⅛ teaspoon of
ground cayenne pepper into the dough.

pizza bites

PREP TIME
10 minutes

COOK TIME
15 minutes

SERVES
6

**TOOLS/
EQUIPMENT**

Cutting board

Knife

Mini muffin pan

Large bowl

Rubber or
silicone spatula

Toothpick

FOR THE BITES

Nonstick cooking spray

1 cup all-purpose flour

1 cup shredded mozzarella

1 cup chopped pepperoni slices

1 cup whole milk

1 large egg

1 teaspoon baking powder

FOR SERVING

Pizza sauce, for dipping

Preheat the oven.

Preheat the oven to 375°F. Spray the cups of a mini muffin pan with cooking spray.

Mix, fill, and bake.

In a large bowl, combine all the pizza bites ingredients and mix with a rubber spatula until blended. Fill each muffin cup three-quarters full with batter. Bake for 12 to 14 minutes, or until puffed and a toothpick inserted into a muffin comes out clean. Serve with pizza sauce for dipping.

TRY INSTEAD If you want to season these with dried basil and oregano or Italian seasoning, go right ahead. You can also make bigger muffins using a traditional-size muffin pan, but increase the cook time to 18 to 20 minutes.

parmesan cheese crisps

**TOOLS/
EQUIPMENT**

Grater (if needed)

Baking sheet

Parchment
paper or silicone
baking mat

8 ounces Parmesan cheese
(pre-shredded or shredded
yourself)

Preheat the oven.

Preheat the oven to 425°F, and line a baking sheet
with parchment paper or a silicone baking mat.

Assemble the crisps.

Place 1½ tablespoons of cheese in a mound on the
prepared baking sheet. Spread the cheese out just
enough to form the shape of a potato chip. Repeat,
leaving about ½ inch between each mound of
cheese, until all the cheese is used.

Bake and serve.

Bake for 3 to 5 minutes, or until the cheese is
golden and crisp. These crisps are best enjoyed
the same day.

PRO TIP Make larger crisps for edible
salad bowls—this works great with
Caesar salad. Place ⅓ cup of cheese on the
prepared baking sheet, and spread into a
5- or 6-inch circle. Bake for 8 to 11 minutes,
or until the cheese has melted and begun
turning golden and light brown in spots.
Working quickly, use a metal spatula to lift the
crisp off the baking sheet and then drape it
over an upside down small bowl or ramekin.
Help shape it into a bowl by pulling the sides
down gently. Let cool completely before using.

crispy baked garlic-parmesan wings

PREP TIME
20 minutes, plus 30 minutes to marinate

COOK TIME
45 minutes

SERVES
4 TO **6**

TOOLS/ EQUIPMENT

Kitchen shears or chef's knife, if separating wings

Cutting board

Grater

Paper towel

2 large bowls

Plastic wrap

Baking sheet

Medium pot

2 pounds chicken wings and drumettes, completely thawed

2 tablespoons olive oil

½ teaspoon kosher salt, plus more for marinating

½ teaspoon freshly ground black pepper, plus more for marinating

½ cup unsalted butter (1 stick)

2 tablespoons garlic paste or 2 large garlic cloves, finely minced

2 tablespoons Buffalo wing sauce

¼ cup chicken stock

1 teaspoon onion powder

¼ cup grated Parmesan cheese

HELPFUL HINT The size of the wings may affect cooking time. Larger wings take longer.

Preseason the wings.

Pat the wings dry with paper towel, place in a large bowl with the olive oil and a pinch of salt and pepper, and toss to coat well. Cover with plastic wrap, and marinate for 30 minutes in the refrigerator.

Bake the wings.

Preheat the oven to 400°F. Spread the wings in a single layer on a baking sheet, and bake for 40 to 45 minutes, or until lightly browned and crisp (see Helpful Hint).

Prepare the sauce.

Meanwhile, in a medium pot, combine the butter, garlic, wing sauce, stock, onion powder, salt, and pepper, and bring to a simmer. Set aside, and reheat if necessary as the wings come out of the oven.

Season and serve.

Place the baked wings in a large bowl, pour in the sauce, and toss the wings to coat. Sprinkle with the Parmesan cheese, and toss again. Serve with plenty of napkins!

ADD-INS For a pop of color, toss the cooked wings with 1 or 2 teaspoons of fresh thyme along with the Parmesan cheese.

PRO TIP Look for party wings that are already separated into wing and drumette sections in the frozen or fresh meat section of your grocer. If the wings are whole, you will need to use kitchen shears or a chef's knife to separate them. Ask an adult for help.

Caprese Grilled Cheese (page 90)

5

soups,
salads &
sandwiches

tortellini & spinach soup

PREP TIME
5 minutes

COOK TIME
15 minutes

SERVES
6

**TOOLS/
EQUIPMENT**
Cutting board
Knife
Large pot
Wooden spoon
Ladle

2 tablespoons olive or grapeseed oil

6 garlic cloves, minced

6 cups chicken broth

20 ounces packaged fresh cheese tortellini

1 (14.5-ounce) can crushed tomatoes

12 ounces baby spinach leaves

Salt (optional)

Freshly ground black pepper (optional)

Make the broth.
In a large pot over medium-high heat, heat the oil. Add the garlic, and sauté for 30 seconds. Add the broth, increase the heat to high, and bring to a boil.

Add the tortellini.
Once the broth is boiling, add the tortellini and cook for half the cooking time on the package directions. Add the tomatoes, reduce the heat to medium-low, and continue cooking until the tortellini is tender.

Wilt the spinach and serve.
Stir in the spinach and cook until it wilts, about a minute. Season with salt and pepper, if needed, ladle into bowls, and serve.

ADD-INS If you like spicy, in the first step add a few shakes of ground cayenne pepper with the chicken broth.

white bean & bacon soup

PREP TIME
10 minutes

COOK TIME
40 minutes, plus
10 minutes to sit

SERVES

4

6 slices bacon, chopped

½ cup diced onion

¼ cup diced carrot

3 garlic cloves, minced

1 tablespoon olive or grapeseed oil

2 (15-ounce) cans cannellini beans
(white beans), drained and rinsed

Dash kosher salt

Dash freshly ground black pepper

2 cups (16 ounces) chicken stock

Crisp the bacon.

In a large pot over medium heat, cook the bacon until crisp, about 8 minutes. Scoop out the bacon, drain it on a paper towel–lined plate, and reserve the fat in the pot.

Add the remaining ingredients.

Add the onion and carrot and sauté in the bacon fat for 5 minutes. Add the garlic and sauté for 1 to 2 minutes, stirring frequently. Add the oil, then add the beans, salt, pepper, and chicken stock, stirring well to blend.

Simmer the soup and serve.

Reduce the heat to medium-low, and simmer for 25 minutes. Then, use a potato masher or the back of a wooden spoon to mash some of the beans to add creaminess to the soup. Turn off the heat and let the soup sit for at least 10 minutes. Ladle the soup into bowls, top each with bacon, and serve.

 HELPFUL HINT This soup reheats well and tastes delicious the following day.

ADD-INS If you like, add ½ tablespoon of dried basil and sprinkle with a little freshly shaved Parmesan cheese before serving.

sweet potato bisque

PREP TIME
10 minutes

COOK TIME
20 minutes

SERVES

4

TOOLS/ EQUIPMENT

Cutting board

Knife

Large pot

Wooden spoon

Immersion blender or blender

Ladle

2 tablespoons olive or grapeseed oil

¾ cup chopped sweet onion

4 cups vegetable or chicken stock

2 heaping cups peeled, diced sweet potatoes or yams (about 2 large)

2 tablespoons brown sugar

¼ teaspoon ground cinnamon

2 pinches kosher salt

Sauté the onion.
In a large pot over medium heat, heat the oil. Add the onion and sauté until wilted and translucent, about 4 minutes.

Cook the potatoes.
Add the stock and sweet potatoes, and simmer, covered, until the potatoes are tender, about 15 minutes. Remove from the heat and allow the soup to cool a bit.

Carefully purée.
Use an immersion blender or carefully pour the soup into a blender and purée. (NOTE: Hot soup can splatter! While blending, place a dish towel over the lid of the blender to avoid splattering.)

Taste, adjust, and serve.
Rinse the pot clean, return the soup to the pot, add the brown sugar, cinnamon, and salt, and taste. If you want it a little sweeter, stir in a bit more brown sugar. Ladle into bowls and serve warm.

ADD-INS If you like spicy, a shake or two of ground cayenne pepper is delicious in this soup. If you like sweet, make cinnamon-sugar croutons to top the soup. Here's how: Dip cubes of bread in melted butter, then dip the cubes in a cinnamon-sugar mixture, and pan-fry on all sides in a little butter until crispy. These can be made ahead and stored in an airtight container.

lemon vinaigrette

**TOOLS/
EQUIPMENT**

Glass jar with
tightly fitting lid

½ cup grapeseed or olive oil

3 tablespoons freshly squeezed lemon
juice or white wine vinegar

1 tablespoon honey

1 teaspoon coarse Dijon mustard

Pinch salt

Pinch freshly ground black pepper

Shake and store.

In a glass jar, combine all the ingredients. Cover
tightly and shake well to blend. Refrigerate until
ready to use. Shake well before using.

ADD-INS You can add 1 minced garlic
clove or 1 minced shallot for an extra
boost of flavor.

TRY INSTEAD Substitute lime juice for
the lemon.

homemade ranch dressing

PREP TIME
10 minutes, plus
1 hour to chill

SERVES
6

**TOOLS/
EQUIPMENT**

Cutting board

Knife

Large bowl

Whisk or
mixing spoon

Container with lid

½ cup mayonnaise

½ cup sour cream

½ cup buttermilk

1 tablespoon chopped fresh dill

1 tablespoon chopped fresh parsley

½ teaspoon garlic powder

¼ teaspoon onion powder

1 teaspoon freshly squeezed
lemon juice

½ teaspoon salt

Dash freshly ground black pepper

Mix ingredients and chill.
In a large bowl, combine all the ingredients and whisk vigorously until combined. Scrape the dressing into a small container, cover, and refrigerate for 1 hour or more to chill and allow the flavors to mingle. Can be refrigerated for up to 7 days.

 TRY INSTEAD If you like some kick in your dressing, add in a swirl or two (or more) of Sriracha and make this Spicy Sriracha Ranch Dressing.

shaved brussels sprouts salad

PREP TIME
20 minutes

SERVES
4

**TOOLS/
EQUIPMENT**

Cutting board

Knife

Grater

Medium bowl

Wooden spoon

Salad tongs

1 pound Brussels sprouts, woody stems removed, grated or shredded (see Pro Tips)

1 large sweet apple, such as Honeycrisp, or tart apple, such as Granny Smith, chopped or cut into thin half-moons

¼ cup raw pepitas (pumpkin seeds), pistachios, or walnut pieces

Lemon Vinaigrette (page 86)

¾ cup or more freshly shaved Parmesan cheese

ADD-INS Add ½ cup of dried cranberries and/or a few paper-thin slices of red onion.

Mix and serve.

In a medium bowl, combine the Brussels sprouts, apples, and pepitas. Toss to combine. Add 3 table-spoons of Lemon Vinaigrette, tossing to coat. Use tongs to transfer the salad to individual serving plates. Sprinkle each plate with shaved Parmesan, and serve with extra dressing on the side.

PRO TIPS Options for shaving Brussels sprouts:

- Use a paring knife. Cut each sprout in half. Lay halves cut-side down so they don't move around, and carefully slice as thinly as you can.
- Use a mandoline. ALWAYS use the protective guard. Another option is piercing each sprout with a fork and moving it back and forth across the blade, keeping fingers clear.
- Use a food processor fitted with a slicing blade. Add the sprouts, a handful at a time, into the chute, and then use the pusher tool to press them down onto the rotating blade.

orzo pesto salad

PREP TIME
10 minutes

COOK TIME
10 minutes

SERVES
6

**TOOLS/
EQUIPMENT**
Cutting board
Knife
Large pot
Colander
Large bowl
Small pot
Mixing spoon

½ pound orzo pasta

1 tablespoon olive or grapeseed oil

1 bunch asparagus

Kosher salt

1 heaping cup halved grape tomatoes

4 scallions, sliced thin

Freshly ground black pepper

4 to 5 tablespoons pesto, store-bought or homemade (see Pro Tip)

Cook the orzo.

In a large pot, cook the orzo according to package directions for al dente (firm). Strain the pasta in a colander, and immediately begin running cold water over it to completely cool it down. Drain it well. Transfer to a large bowl, toss with the oil, and set aside.

Cook the asparagus.

Slice the tips off the asparagus, then cut another 1-inch piece off of each spear, reserving the rest of the asparagus for another use. Fill a small pot half-way with water, salt the water (about 1 tablespoon), and bring to a boil. Add the asparagus pieces and blanch for 1 to 2 minutes, until crisp-tender. Drain the asparagus tips in a colander, and immediately run under cold water to stop the cooking process.

Mix the ingredients and serve.

Add the asparagus, tomatoes, and scallions to the bowl with the orzo. Season with salt and pepper, and toss to mix. Add the pesto, toss again to coat, and serve.

 TROUBLESHOOTING If making ahead of time, refresh the salad with a tablespoon of pesto or olive oil just before serving.

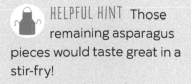 HELPFUL HINT Those remaining asparagus pieces would taste great in a stir-fry!

PRO TIP It's easy to make your own pesto. Just add 1 cup of fresh basil, 2 garlic cloves, 2 tablespoons of pine nuts, ¼ cup of olive oil, salt, and pepper to a food processor or high-powered blender and pulse until smooth. Scrape the pesto into a small bowl, and stir in ¼ cup of grated Parmesan cheese. Cover and refrigerate until ready to use.

caprese grilled cheese

PREP TIME
10 minutes

COOK TIME
5 minutes

SERVES
4

**TOOLS/
EQUIPMENT**
Cutting board
Serrated knife
Butter knife
Large skillet
Metal spatula

Mayonnaise, for spreading

8 thick slices sourdough bread

2 large ripe tomatoes, cut into
8 slices total

Salt

Freshly ground black pepper

Handful fresh basil leaves

8 slices fresh mozzarella cheese

2 tablespoons butter, at room
temperature, divided

Assemble the sandwiches.

Spread the mayonnaise on one side of each piece of bread; top each with 2 slices of tomato. Season the tomatoes with salt and pepper. Top the tomatoes with the basil, then 2 slices each of mozzarella.

Cook the sandwiches, slice, and serve.

In a large skillet over medium heat, melt 1 tablespoon of butter, tipping the skillet to spread the butter. Place the sandwiches on the skillet two at a time. Cook until the bread facing down is golden brown, about 3 minutes. Add another tablespoon of butter, then carefully flip the sandwiches over and cook until golden brown, about 3 minutes longer. Remove the pan from the heat and allow the sandwiches to sit for another minute, until the cheese is gooey. Slice and serve.

TRY INSTEAD Instead of using fresh basil, use pesto (see Pro Tip, page 89), spreading it onto each slice of bread. If you like grilled cheese the old-fashioned way, just swap the ingredients for American or Cheddar cheese slices and cook it the same way!

asian noodle salad

PREP TIME
15 minutes

COOK TIME
10 minutes

SERVES

8 TO 10

**TOOLS/
EQUIPMENT**

Cutting board

Knife

Glass jar with lid

Large pot

Wooden spoon

Strainer or
colander

Paper towels

Tongs (optional)

Serving bowl

FOR THE SAUCE

½ cup soy sauce

3 tablespoons sesame oil

2 tablespoons red wine vinegar or rice
wine vinegar

2 tablespoons olive oil

1 tablespoon plus 1 teaspoon sugar

1½ tablespoons chili sauce with garlic

FOR THE SALAD

1 pound linguine

1 red pepper, sliced thin
into 1- to 2-inch-long pieces

4 or 5 scallions, sliced thin

Make the sauce.

In a jar with a lid, combine all the sauce ingredients.
Cover and shake vigorously to mix well.

Cook the pasta.

In a large pot, cook the pasta according to package
directions for for al dente (firm).

Prep the noodles.

Drain the noodles, then run under cold water until
cool. Shake as much water out as you can, then
blot the noodles dry with paper towels. Dry the pot,
return the noodles to the pot, and pour half the
sauce over them. Toss with tongs or clean hands to
coat every noodle.

Complete the dish.

Add in most of the peppers and scallions, and toss
to mix. Transfer to a serving bowl. Arrange the rest
of the peppers and scallions on top, and pour the
remaining sauce over top. Cover and let stand at
room temperature until ready to serve.

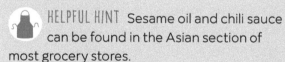 HELPFUL HINT Sesame oil and chili sauce
can be found in the Asian section of
most grocery stores.

TROUBLESHOOTING If you are making this
ahead of time, it can dry out a bit, so
make some extra sauce to freshen it up just
prior to serving. Simply increase sauce ingredients by 50 percent and store extra sauce in a
jar or covered container until ready to use.

cobb salad

TOOLS/
EQUIPMENT

Cutting board

Chef's knife

Large bowl or
4 small bowls

1 head iceberg lettuce or 2 romaine hearts, stems removed, torn into bite-size pieces

1½ cups chopped grape tomatoes

1½ cups cooked crumbled bacon

2 avocados, peeled, pitted, and sliced

3 large hard-boiled eggs, chopped

Homemade Ranch Dressing (page 87) or favorite dressing, for serving

TROUBLESHOOTING Avocados brown quickly, so they should be prepared and added as close to serving as possible. The bacon is also added just before serving so it will stay crispy.

Assemble the salad and serve.

Put the lettuce in 1 large salad bowl or divide evenly among 4 individual bowls. Top with the ingredients, giving each their own "row" next to one another atop the lettuce: a row of tomatoes, a row of bacon, a row of avocados, and a row of eggs. Serve immediately, along with Homemade Ranch Dressing (page 87) or your favorite dressing.

ADD-INS To make this dish more filling, you can add 1½ cups of cubed grilled chicken breast, shredded cheese, or blue cheese, giving each its own row.

PRO TIP The opinions are endless on how to make perfect hard-boiled eggs. Here's my preference: Place the eggs in a medium pot, and cover by 2 inches with cool water. Boil the eggs over high heat. Once the water is vigorously boiling, reduce the heat to medium. After 9 minutes, remove the pot from the stove, move it to the sink, carefully dump out as much of the hot water as possible, and run the eggs under cold water to halt the cooking process. I like a little moistness in my yolks, so 9 minutes for large eggs is what works for me. If you want yours fully dry, cook for 12 to 14 minutes.

asian lettuce wraps

PREP TIME
10 minutes

COOK TIME
15 minutes

SERVES
4

**TOOLS/
EQUIPMENT**
Cutting board
Knife
Medium pot
Mixing spoon
Small bowl
Whisk
Serving platter
Serving bowl

1 tablespoon olive oil

½ cup diced sweet onion

1 tablespoon minced garlic

1 pound ground chicken

¼ cup soy sauce

¼ cup ketchup

1 tablespoon sesame oil

3 tablespoons brown sugar

1 head iceberg lettuce, core removed, separated into leaves

Shredded carrots, sliced scallion, and sliced radish, for serving

Cook the filling.

In a medium pot over medium-high heat, heat the olive oil. Add the onion, and sauté for 2 minutes. Add the garlic, and sauté for another minute. Add the chicken and cook, breaking apart with a spoon, until no longer pink, 4 to 5 minutes.

Prepare the sauce.

In a small bowl, whisk together the soy sauce, ketchup, sesame oil, and brown sugar. Add the sauce to the chicken mixture, and bring to a simmer. Turn off the heat.

Serve family-style.

Serve the lettuce leaves and sliced vegetables on a platter and the chicken mixture in a bowl. Let everyone place a scoop of chicken mixture into a leaf, roll it or fold it in half, and enjoy!

ADD-INS Try this dish with ½ cup of cocktail peanuts for a delicious crunch. If you like a little heat, add 1 tablespoon of chili sauce with garlic and/or ½ to 1 teaspoon of red pepper flakes.

TRY INSTEAD Instead of eating this as a wrap, you can make it into a lettuce bowl: shred the lettuce, place it in bowls, and top with the chicken mixture.

chicken salad wraps

PREP TIME
15 minutes

SERVES
4

**TOOLS/
EQUIPMENT**

Cutting board

Knife

Food processor

Rubber spatula

Large bowl

Heaping ½ cup coarsely
chopped carrots

1½ stalks celery, cut into 1-inch chunks

1½ pounds chicken meat, from
a rotisserie chicken or cooked
chicken breasts

½ to ¾ cup mayonnaise

Salt

Freshly ground black pepper

4 flour tortilla wraps

Lettuce, for serving

Pulse the ingredients.
In a food processor, pulse the carrots and celery
until minced. Chop or tear the chicken into 1-inch
chunks, add to the food processor, and pulse a few
times until chopped. Add the mayonnaise, salt and
pepper to taste, and pulse until combined. Taste
and adjust if needed. Scrape the chicken salad into
a large bowl.

Assemble the wraps and serve.
Place a couple leaves of lettuce onto each wrap,
add a dollop of chicken salad, roll up burrito-style,
and serve.

TRY INSTEAD Add a little honey with the
mayonnaise for sweetness. You can add
some jalapeño if you enjoy heat, or cooked
bacon crumbles to make it even more delicious. You can also use plain Greek yogurt in
place of the mayonnaise.

blackened tuna sandwiches

PREP TIME
10 minutes, plus
15 minutes to sit

COOK TIME
5 minutes

SERVES
2

TOOLS/ EQUIPMENT

Cutting board

Knife

Small bowl

Large nonstick skillet or sauté pan

Metal spatula

¼ cup mayonnaise

Handful fresh basil, chopped

2 (6-ounce) fresh tuna steaks

3 tablespoons blackening seasoning

2 to 3 tablespoons olive or grapeseed oil

2 round rolls

Lettuce leaves

Sliced tomato

Prep the ingredients.

Let the tuna sit at room temperature for 15 minutes. Meanwhile, in a small bowl, mix the mayonnaise and basil. Set aside.

Cook the tuna.

Generously coat the tuna in the blackening seasoning. In a large, nonstick sauté pan or skillet over medium-high heat, heat the oil. Once very hot, add the tuna steaks and cook for 3 minutes on each side for medium. Add additional oil to the pan if the pan looks dry.

Assemble the sandwiches and serve.

Slice open the rolls horizontally, and spread the cut sides of the rolls with the basil mayonnaise. Place some lettuce and a tomato slice on the bottom half of each roll. Top each with a cooked tuna steak and serve.

HELPFUL HINT Decide how well cooked you enjoy your tuna and adjust the cook time; either shorter or longer by 30 seconds to 1 minute per side. Cook time will also vary depending on the thickness of the tuna steaks.

Lemon Chicken (page 106)

main dishes

veggie fried rice

PREP TIME
10 minutes

COOK TIME
10 minutes

SERVES
4

**TOOLS/
EQUIPMENT**

Cutting board

Knife

Large sauté
pan or wok

Spatula

Serving bowl

1 tablespoon sesame oil

½ cup chopped sweet onion

½ cup frozen peas and carrots

1 large egg, lightly beaten

1½ cups cooked rice

2 tablespoons soy sauce

3 tablespoons chopped scallions

Cook the veggies.
In a large skillet or wok over medium-high heat, heat the oil. Once the oil is hot, add the onion and peas and carrots mixture, and cook for 4 to 5 minutes, or until tender.

Scramble the egg.
Using a spatula, push the vegetable mixture to the side of the pan. Add the beaten egg, and scramble it in the pan. Once the egg is cooked through, mix the vegetables into the egg. Add the rice, stirring to incorporate. Add the soy sauce, and stir thoroughly, cooking until heated through.

Garnish and serve.
Transfer the rice to a serving bowl, sprinkle the scallions over top, and serve.

TRY INSTEAD You can make this into Bacon Fried Rice. Just cook chopped bacon in a large skillet over medium-high heat until crisp, about 8 minutes. Remove the bacon and follow the recipe steps, using the bacon fat in place of the oil. Crumble the bacon into the rice before serving.

spaghetti aglio e olio

PREP TIME
10 minutes

COOK TIME
20 minutes, plus
3 minutes to sit

SERVES
4

**TOOLS/
EQUIPMENT**
Cutting board
Knife
Grater
Large skillet
Wooden spoon
Large pot
Colander or
strainer
Serving dish

⅓ cup olive or grapeseed oil

5 large garlic cloves, sliced very thin

1 pound spaghetti or linguini

Kosher salt

Freshly ground black pepper

1 cup freshly grated Parmesan
cheese, divided

⅓ cup chopped fresh parsley, divided

 **TROUBLESHOOTING** You
can cook the pasta
first, toss it with the ingredients in the fourth step (**Mix
the pasta and sauce**), and
wait for the sauce to finish.
The hot sauce will quickly
heat the pasta, while the oil
on it prevents any sticking.

Cook the garlic.
In a large skillet over low heat, heat the oil. Add the garlic, and sauté until golden brown, 3 to 4 minutes. Remove from the heat and set aside.

Cook the pasta.
Using well salted water, cook the pasta according to package directions for al dente (firm). Once the pasta is done and ready to be drained, scoop out 1 cup of the cooking water and add it to the skillet with the garlic. Drain the pasta.

Make the sauce.
Heat the skillet with the water and garlic over medium-high heat, season with salt and pepper, stir to mix, and bring the mixture to a boil for 3 minutes.

Mix the pasta and sauce.
Meanwhile, return the pasta to the pot. Add the olive oil, season with salt and pepper, add about half the cheese and half the parsley, and toss well to combine. As soon as the sauce has been at a boil for 3 minutes, carefully pour the sauce into the pot with the pasta and toss. Let sit for 3 minutes for the flavors to mingle.

Garnish and serve.
Scrape the pasta into a serving dish, top with the remaining cheese and parsley, and serve.

 ADD-INS For spiciness, add a dash of red pepper flakes.

ravioli lasagna

PREP TIME
10 minutes

COOK TIME
45 minutes,
plus 10 minutes
to rest

SERVES

6

**TOOLS/
EQUIPMENT**

Grater

8-by-8-inch
baking dish

Aluminum foil

Nonstick cooking spray

2 cups pasta sauce

24 to 30 ounces frozen cheese
ravioli, divided

½ cup grated Parmesan cheese

1½ cups shredded mozzarella cheese

Preheat the oven.

Preheat the oven to 375°F, and spray an 8-by-8-inch baking dish with cooking spray.

Layer and bake.

Spread a layer of pasta sauce across the bottom of the baking dish, and cover the sauce with an even layer of ravioli. Top with about half each of the remaining sauce, Parmesan cheese, and mozzarella. Top the cheese with a second layer of ravioli, and top with the remaining sauce and cheeses. Cover with foil and bake for 35 to 45 minutes, until the pasta is tender, removing the foil during the last 10 minutes of cooking. Allow to rest for 10 to 15 minutes before serving.

 ADD-INS Add a layer (2 cups) of baby spinach leaves atop the first layer of ravioli.

skillet chicken thighs

PREP TIME
10 minutes

COOK TIME
15 minutes

SERVES
4

**TOOLS/
EQUIPMENT**

Small bowl

Whisk

Paper towel

Large
nonstick skillet

Tongs

Spatula

Meat
thermometer

2 tablespoons apple cider vinegar
or white wine vinegar

2 tablespoons soy sauce

2 tablespoons pure maple syrup

8 boneless chicken thighs

Kosher salt

Freshly ground black pepper

2 tablespoons olive or grapeseed oil

Fresh thyme, for garnish (optional)

DID YOU KNOW? Chicken thighs are juicier than chicken breasts—and less expensive, too!

Make the sauce.
In a small bowl, whisk together the vinegar, soy sauce, and maple syrup. Set aside.

Prepare the chicken.
Blot the chicken thighs dry with a paper towel, and season generously with salt and pepper.

Cook the chicken.
In a large nonstick skillet over medium-high heat, heat the oil until shimmering. Using tongs, add the chicken thighs one at a time (the pan should sizzle as you add them). Cook for about 4 minutes on one side to brown the skin. Turn them over and cook for an additional 4 minutes. Once both sides of the thighs are browned, pour in the sauce. When the sauce begins to bubble, reduce the heat to medium and continue cooking, flipping the thighs every minute or so. Once the sauce has thickened, after about 5 minutes, check the thighs for doneness; a meat thermometer inserted into the thickest part of the thigh should read 165°F when done (see Helpful Hint).

Garnish and serve.
Sprinkle with fresh thyme, if desired, and serve.

HELPFUL HINT Cook time will vary based on the size of thighs. Larger pieces will take a bit longer.

chicken cheese meatballs

PREP TIME
10 minutes,
plus 30 minutes
to chill

COOK TIME
20 minutes

SERVES
4

**TOOLS/
EQUIPMENT**
Cutting board
Knife
Rimmed
baking sheet
Large bowl
Spatula
Plastic wrap
Medium
casserole dish

Nonstick cooking spray or olive oil

1 pound ground chicken

1 garlic clove, minced,
or 1 tablespoon garlic paste

½ cup bread crumbs

Salt

Freshly ground black pepper

1 large egg

2 tablespoons fresh basil, chopped,
or 1 tablespoon dried basil

16 ounces pasta sauce

1 cup fresh or shredded
mozzarella cheese

Preheat the oven.
Preheat the oven to 375°F. Spray a baking sheet with cooking spray or lightly coat with olive oil.

Mix the ingredients.
In a large bowl, combine the chicken, garlic, bread crumbs, salt, pepper, egg, and basil. Mix with clean hands or a spatula until combined. Cover with plastic wrap and refrigerate for 30 minutes.

Form the meatballs and bake.
Using clean hands, form the chicken mixture into meatballs. Arrange the meatballs, not touching each nother, on the prepared baking sheet. Bake for 10 to 12 minutes, until they begin to brown.

Assemble the dish and serve.
Pour the pasta sauce into a medium casserole dish. Place the baked meatballs in the dish, turning to coat with sauce. Top each meatball with a slice of mozzarella or a mound of shredded cheese. Return to the oven and cook for an additional 7 to 10 minutes, or until the sauce is bubbly and the cheese is melted. Serve hot.

TRY INSTEAD Make Buffalo Chicken Meatballs. Omit the basil. After the meatballs bake the first time, place them in a medium pot with your favorite buffalo wing sauce (look for sauce marked "wing sauce," not "hot sauce"). Simmer on low for 10 minutes and serve.

lemon chicken

PREP TIME
10 minutes

COOK TIME
10 minutes

SERVES
4

TOOLS/ EQUIPMENT
Cutting board
Knife
Grater (optional)
Wax paper
Mallet, rolling pin, or heavy pan
Shallow bowl
Plate
Large skillet
Spatula
Meat thermometer

4 boneless chicken breasts

2 teaspoons lemon-pepper seasoning

⅓ cup all-purpose flour

3 tablespoons butter

2 lemons, 1 sliced thinly into rounds, and the other juiced

2 tablespoons chopped or snipped fresh parsley

Lemon zest, for serving (optional)

Pound the chicken.

Place the chicken breasts between two pieces of wax paper. Using a mallet, pound the chicken to about ½-inch thickness. Season on both sides with the lemon-pepper seasoning.

Coat the chicken.

Spread the flour in a shallow bowl, and, one by one, dredge the chicken breasts until evenly coated. Place the coated chicken on a plate.

Cook the chicken.

In a large skillet over medium-high heat, melt the butter. Add the chicken in batches, and cook for 3 to 6 minutes on each side (depending on size and thickness, until the internal temperature reaches 165°F on a meat thermometer). After you flip the chicken, add the lemon juice, swirling the pan around gently to distribute.

Garnish and serve.

Remove the chicken from the pan, pour any remaining sauce over the chicken, garnish with the parsley, lemon slices, and a little bit of lemon zest if desired, and serve.

> ADD-INS Like the taste of olives? Add 1 tablespoon of caper juice and 2 to 3 tablespoons of capers to the chicken while it cooks.

chicken italiano

PREP TIME
10 minutes

COOK TIME
20 minutes

SERVES
4

**TOOLS/
EQUIPMENT**

Large
nonstick skillet

Tongs or spatula

Small pot

Meat
thermometer

4 (6-ounce) skinless, boneless
chicken breasts

Salt

Freshly ground black pepper

Olive oil

2 cups pasta sauce

4 (½-inch-thick) slices fresh
mozzarella cheese

4 large pieces jarred or fresh roasted
red peppers

Chopped fresh parsley (optional)

Preheat the oven.
Preheat the oven to 375°F.

Season the chicken.
Season the chicken breasts with salt and pepper,
and set aside.

Cook the chicken and heat the sauce.
Pour enough oil into a large nonstick skillet to just
cover the bottom. Heat over medium-high heat
until the oil is shimmering. Cook the chicken, turning
once, until the outside is browned and the chicken
is cooked through, 4 to 6 minutes per side depending on size, or until the internal temperature reaches
165°F on a meat thermometer. Meanwhile, in a small
pot over medium heat, heat the pasta sauce.

Assemble the dish.
Once the chicken is done cooking, place a slice of
mozzarella on each piece of chicken, followed by
a slice of roasted red pepper. Place the stacks in
the skillet over medium-low heat for 3 to 5 minutes,
until the cheese begins to melt. Spoon warm pasta
sauce onto individual plates, place a stack on top,
add a little more sauce over top, garnish with a little
chopped parsley, if desired, and serve.

> HELPFUL HINTS Cook time will vary
> based on the size and thickness of
> the chicken. If the chicken breasts are large
> and thick, slice them horizontally to create
> thinner breasts.

stuffed chicken breasts

PREP TIME
15 minutes

COOK TIME
35 minutes

SERVES
6

**TOOLS/
EQUIPMENT**
Cutting board
Chef's knife
Baking sheet or
large baking dish
Medium bowl
Meat
thermometer

Nonstick cooking spray

6 to 8 boneless chicken breasts

Salt

Freshly ground black pepper

1 (10-ounce) box frozen chopped
spinach, thawed

1 (8-ounce block) cream cheese,
room temperature

4 scallions, chopped

⅓ cup grainy Dijon mustard

 TROUBLESHOOTING
If you are making this
ahead, add the mustard just
before baking.

Preheat the oven.
Preheat the oven to 350°F, and coat a baking sheet
or baking dish with cooking spray.

Prepare the chicken.
Trim any fat off of each chicken breast, and season
with salt and pepper. Carefully slice a "pocket" into
each breast by slicing on the diagonal through the
breast, almost halving it but leaving one side and
bottom and edge intact, like a flap. Set aside.

Mix the stuffing.
In small handfuls, squeeze all the water from the
spinach. In a medium bowl, combine the spinach,
cream cheese, and scallions, and season with additional salt and pepper. Mix well, using clean hands if
necessary.

Stuff and bake.
Stuff each breast with plenty of the mixture. Pack
it in, press it down, and pull the flap over the top.
Place on the baking sheet. Spread the mustard over
top of each breast. Bake for 25 to 30 minutes until
the meat is firm and opaque, any juices run clear,
and a meat thermometer inserted in the thickest
part of the breast, registers 165°F. Cook time will
vary based on the thickness of the chicken breasts.

HELPFUL HINTS Whenever you are
working with raw chicken, be sure to
thoroughly wash your cutting board afterward
with very warm soapy water. Always wash your
hands after handling raw chicken or meat, and
thoroughly wipe down your counter.

garlicky sautéed mussels

PREP TIME
10 minutes

COOK TIME
10 minutes

SERVES
2

TOOLS/ EQUIPMENT

Cutting board

Knife

Large skillet with lid

Slotted spoon or tongs

Shallow serving dish

2 tablespoons butter

3 large garlic cloves, minced

⅓ cup white wine

2 pounds mussels or 30 littleneck clams, scrubbed clean and rinsed well in a bowl of cold water

1 tablespoon freshly squeezed lemon juice

2 tablespoons fresh parsley, minced

Freshly ground black pepper

Cook the shellfish.

In a large skillet over medium heat, melt the butter. Add the garlic. When the garlic begins to sizzle, add the wine and shellfish. Increase the heat to high, cover, and steam, shaking the pan back and forth occasionally to allow even cooking until all mussels or clams have opened, about 5 minutes for mussels, and 6 minutes for clams. Discard any that do not open.

Season and serve.

Using a slotted spoon or tongs, transfer the shellfish to a shallow serving dish, reserving the broth. Add the lemon juice to the broth, then add the parsley and season with black pepper. Pour the broth over the shellfish and serve.

ADD-INS You can also add some crumbled cooked chorizo sausage to the hot broth with the shellfish. Add a pinch or two of ground cayenne or red pepper flakes for a little spicy heat.

garlic shrimp

PREP TIME
15 minutes

COOK TIME
5 minutes

SERVES

4

**TOOLS/
EQUIPMENT**

Cutting board

Knife

Large sauté pan

Spatula

3 tablespoons olive oil

8 garlic cloves, chopped

2 pounds large shrimp (21 to 25 count),
cleaned, shells and tails removed

Kosher salt

Freshly ground black pepper

1 stick butter, cut into 6 chunks, divided

⅓ cup freshly squeezed lemon juice

¼ cup capers, and a splash of
caper juice

Ground cayenne pepper

2 tablespoons chopped fresh parsley

Cook the shrimp.
In a large sauté pan over medium-high heat, heat
the oil. Add the garlic and sauté for 30 seconds.
Add the shrimp and sauté for 1 to 2 minutes.
Reduce the heat to medium, and sprinkle with salt
and black pepper.

Season and cook through.
Add 3 chunks of butter and the lemon juice, and
continue to cook, turning occasionally, until no
longer pink and cooked through, about 2 more
minutes.

Garnish and serve.
Remove from the heat, add the capers and juice,
sprinkle with the cayenne pepper and parsley, and
add the remaining 3 chunks of butter. Toss until the
butter is melted, and serve immediately.

sticky honey-lime salmon

PREP TIME
5 minutes

COOK TIME
10 minutes

SERVES
4

**TOOLS/
EQUIPMENT**
Cutting board
Knife
Small bowl
Whisk
Large nonstick
sauté pan or skillet
Metal spatula
Large fork
Serving plate

¼ cup honey

3 tablespoons low-sodium soy sauce

1 tablespoon freshly squeezed
lime juice

2 garlic cloves, minced

4 skinless salmon fillets

Kosher salt

Freshly ground black pepper

1 to 2 tablespoons olive oil

Chopped scallions, for garnish
(optional)

Make the sauce.

In a small bowl, whisk together the honey, soy sauce, lime juice, and garlic. Set aside.

Cook the salmon.

Season the salmon fillets generously with salt and pepper. In a large nonstick sauté pan or skillet over medium-high heat, heat the olive oil until hot. Add the salmon and reduce the heat to medium. Cook for 3 to 4 minutes. Gently flip the fillets and cook for about 2 minutes more, until seared. Reduce the heat to low, and pour the sauce mixture onto the fillets. Continue to cook for 45 to 60 seconds, and gently flip the fillets to coat the other side in the sauce. Remove from the heat if necessary to allow the sauce to cool down (see Troubleshooting). Remove from the heat when the salmon is cooked to your liking. It should flake easily with a fork. Cook time will vary based on the thickness of the salmon fillets.

Glaze and serve.

Transfer the fillets to a serving plate, reserving the sauce in the pan. Simmer the remaining sauce for another 30 to 60 seconds and spoon over the fillets. Garnish with scallions, if desired, and serve.

 TROUBLESHOOTING The honey in the sauce can cause it to burn easily. Watch it closely while cooking the salmon; if it starts to smoke or darken in color, take it off the heat to cool down a bit before returning the pan to the stove top.

HELPFUL HINT Look for skinless salmon fillets. If not available, skin-on salmon works as well; just cook the skin side first. Press down on the fillets with a spatula during the cooking process, including sides and edges. Skin-on salmon will take a little longer to cook. Cook time should be mostly on the skin side, flipping to just sear the skinless side.

sausage-stuffed zucchini

PREP TIME
15 minutes

COOK TIME
30 minutes

SERVES

4

**TOOLS/
EQUIPMENT**
Cutting board
Chef's knife
Grater
Teaspoon
Large, rimmed
baking sheet
Large
nonstick skillet

2 large zucchini

Salt

Freshly ground black pepper

Homemade Breakfast Sausage
(page 45) or 1 (12-ounce) package
breakfast sausage patties or links

⅓ cup chopped Vidalia (sweet) onion

1 cup chopped pepper (green, red,
or poblano work well)

⅓ cup chopped grape tomatoes

2 cups shredded mozzarella
cheese, divided

Preheat the oven.
Preheat the oven to 375°F.

Prepare the zucchini.
Halve the zucchini lengthwise, and using a teaspoon, scrape out half to three-quarters of the
insides, scraping out all of the seeds. Place the
zucchini, flat-side down, on a large, rimmed baking sheet.

Bake the zucchini.
Bake for 15 minutes. Remove from the oven, flip
the zucchini over, and season the insides with salt
and pepper.

Cook the sausage.
Meanwhile, cut each sausage piece into quarters. In
a large nonstick skillet over medium-high heat, cook
the sausage for 3 minutes, turning occasionally. Add
3 tablespoons of water and the onion and pepper
to the pan.

Cook the veggies.
Continue to simmer until the sausage is cooked
through and the pepper and onion are soft, about
7 minutes. Add the tomatoes, and cook for another
minute. Remove from the heat, add ½ cup of
cheese, and stir until incorporated.

TRY INSTEAD Add some chopped jalapeño or red pepper flakes to kick up the heat. You can also swap half of the mozzarella cheese for shredded Cheddar, blending the two together for a different flavor.

Fill the zucchini.

Fill the zucchini with the vegetable mixture, and top with the remaining 1½ cups of cheese. Bake for 3 minutes, or until the cheese is melted, cool slightly, and serve.

TROUBLESHOOTING I prefer zucchini to be cooked crisp-tender; I don't like it very soft. Cooking time will vary based on the size of your zucchini, how much zucchini you scrape out, and your preference for doneness.

cuban mojo pork

PREP TIME
10 minutes,
plus 2 hours
to marinate

COOK TIME
25 minutes

SERVES
6

**TOOLS/
EQUIPMENT**

Microplane
or zester

Food processor
or blender

Shallow
baking dish

Grill (see
Helpful Hint for
alternative)

Knife

½ cup grapeseed or olive oil

¾ cup freshly squeezed orange juice,
plus the zest of 2 oranges, zested, then
juiced (¾ cup)

¼ cup freshly squeezed lime juice

Large handful fresh cilantro
(about ½ cup)

4 tablespoons garlic paste
or 4 garlic cloves

1 tablespoon fresh oregano leaves

12 fresh mint leaves

Kosher salt

Freshly ground black pepper

3 pounds pork tenderloin
(typically 2 pieces in a package,
each weighing 1¼ to 1½ pounds)

Blend the marinade.

In a food processor or blender, combine the oil,
orange juice, lime juice, cilantro, garlic, oregano,
and mint, and pulse until the leaves and garlic
are minced and the marinade is liquid. Toss in the
orange zest, and stir to combine.

Marinate the pork.

Season the pork with salt and pepper, place in a
shallow baking dish, and pour the marinade over
top. Cover and refrigerate for 2 to 24 hours, turning
the pork occasionally to coat in the marinade.

> NOTE This recipe is best cooked on a
> grill; the char marks are delicious
> mingling with the marinated meat. Ask an
> adult to grill it for you or teach you about
> the grill and how to use it.

Cook the pork.

Make sure the grill is clean and oiled. Preheat the grill to medium-high, and place the pork directly onto the grates. Discard the marinade. Once grill marks appear on the bottom and the meat releases itself, after 3 to 4 minutes, turn the meat a quarter turn. Continue to cook, turning occasionally, for 12 to 14 minutes more. Pork is done when the internal temperature at the thickest part of the tenderloins is 145°F (see Pro Tip). Remove from the grill, tent with foil, and let rest for 5 minutes. Slice and serve.

steak tacos

PREP TIME
25 minutes

COOK TIME
10 minutes, plus
10 minutes
to rest

SERVES

6

**TOOLS/
EQUIPMENT**

1 small bowl and
1 medium bowl

Grater

Large skillet or
sauté pan

Meat
thermometer

Tongs

Cutting board

Chef's knife

½ tablespoon salt

1 teaspoon chili powder

1 teaspoon onion powder

½ teaspoon freshly ground
black pepper

1½ pounds flank steak

2 to 3 carrots

1 small red cabbage

Lemon Vinaigrette (page 86)

½ tablespoon grapeseed or olive oil,
plus more if needed

½ recipe Avocado Dip (page 73) or
guacamole, plus more for serving

Flour tortillas, for serving

Chips, for serving

Rub the steak.

In a small bowl, combine the salt, chili powder, onion powder, and pepper, and mix until blended. Rub the seasoning mix onto both sides of the steak, and allow the steak to sit at room temperature for 20 minutes.

Make the slaw.

Using the larger side of a grater, shred the carrots by holding the carrot on an angle for longer shreds (you should have about 1½ cups). Place the shredded carrots in a medium bowl. Quarter a small head of red cabbage, remove the core from one of the quarters. Slice the quarter crosswise into thin strips and place in the bowl with the carrots (you should have about 1 cup). Toss with the Lemon Vinaigrette, and, using your hands, massage the dressing into the shredded vegetables a bit. Set aside and allow the flavors to mingle.

Fry the steak.

In a large skillet or sauté pan over medium-high heat, heat the oil. Once the oil begins to shimmer and a first wisp of smoke comes off of it, carefully place the steak in the pan. Cook the steak until a meat thermometer registers 145°F for medium (see chart on page 29), typically 4 to 5 minutes per side, turning once with tongs. Add additional oil if the pan looks dry, and reduce the heat if the meat is starting to burn.

Rest and slice.

Transfer the steak to a cutting board and allow to rest for 10 minutes. Using a chef's knife or serrated bread knife, slice the steak into thin slices, going against the grain (see Pro Tip).

Serve and enjoy.

Assemble the tacos by placing the meat, Avocado Dip, and the vegetable slaw onto tortillas. Serve chips alongside with extra Avocado Dip.

PRO TIP Cutting against the grain means to look for the lines that go across the steak in one direction. You will not cut along those lines; for a good cut, cut across those lines.

chimichurri steak

PREP TIME
15 minutes,
plus 20 minutes
to rest

COOK TIME
10 minutes,
plus 10 minutes
to rest

SERVES

4

**TOOLS/
EQUIPMENT**

Cutting board

Knife

Paper towel

Food processor or
high-powered
blender

Small bowl

Large, heavy skillet
or cast-iron pan

Tongs

Meat
thermometer

Serving plate

4 pieces strip steak, rib eye steak,
or fillet steaks

½ teaspoon kosher salt, plus more
for seasoning the steak

¼ teaspoon freshly ground black
pepper, plus more for seasoning
the steak

5 garlic cloves, chopped

2 tablespoons fresh oregano leaves

1 teaspoon red pepper flakes

¼ cup chopped fresh parsley

¼ cup chopped fresh cilantro

3 tablespoons red wine vinegar

½ cup grapeseed or olive oil,
plus more if needed

Prepare the steaks.

Pat the steaks dry with a paper towel. Season well
with kosher salt and pepper, and set aside to rest at
room temperature for 20 to 30 minutes.

Blend the sauce.

In a food processor or high-powered blender,
combine the garlic, oregano, red pepper flakes,
parsley, cilantro, and vinegar. Pulse until the garlic
and greens are finely chopped and the sauce is
blended. Pour into a small bowl and set aside.

Cook the steaks.

In a large, heavy skillet or cast-iron pan over
medium-high heat, heat the oil. Swirl the oil around
to coat the pan. Once the oil begins to shimmer and
the first wisp of smoke appears, add the steaks,
leaving room in between. Cook for 3 to 5 minutes
on one side (see Helpful Hint), then use tongs to
turn the steaks over and cook to desired doneness
or until a meat thermometer inserted in the thickest
part of the steak reads 145°F, for medium (see chart
on page 29). Add more oil if the pan looks dry.

TRY INSTEAD If you do not enjoy the taste of cilantro, simply leave it out. You can also substitute 1 tablespoon of dried oregano for fresh; however, the fresh really helps make the Chimichurri "sing." If you enjoy heat, feel free to add in an additional ½ to 1 teaspoon of red pepper flakes. This sauce is also delicious served over grilled or roasted potatoes.

Rest the steaks and serve.

Remove the steaks from the pan and allow them to rest for 5 to 10 minutes without touching them. Transfer the steaks to a serving plate, spoon a line of chimichurri sauce down the middle of each, and serve.

HELPFUL HINT Thinner steaks will need about 3 minutes on each side for medium doneness, while thicker steaks will need 4 minutes or more on each side, depending on thickness and preferred doneness (see chart, page 29).

PRO TIP Never flip steak with a fork—you don't want to pierce the meat and allow juices to escape! Always use tongs to flip steak. And be sure to let steaks rest after cooking for best results.

Flourless Chocolate Cake (page 139)

desserts

watermelon-lime sorbet

PREP TIME
10 minutes,
plus 6 hours
to freeze

COOK TIME
1 minute

SERVES

6

**TOOLS/
EQUIPMENT**

Baking sheet

Parchment paper
or wax paper

Small pot

Food processor
or high-powered
blender

6 cups cubed watermelon

¼ cup water

3 tablespoons sugar

¼ cup freshly squeezed lime juice
(2 to 3 limes)

HELPFUL HINT Water-
melons vary in both
sweetness and water content.
If your watermelon is very
sweet, you may not even
choose to add the sugar
mixture.

Freeze the watermelon.

Line a baking sheet with parchment paper or wax
paper. Spread the watermelon cubes on the baking
sheet, and freeze for 30 minutes. Transfer the cubes
to a freezer-safe container in the freezer for at least
6 hours or overnight.

Make the sorbet.

When ready to make the sorbet, make a simple
syrup by heating the water and sugar in a small pot
over medium heat and stirring. Once the sugar is
dissolved, remove from the heat. Place the frozen
watermelon and lime juice in a food processor or
high-powered blender, drizzle in the warm simple
syrup, and blend until the watermelon breaks down
into an icy slush. Enjoy immediately or freeze for
30 minutes.

PRO TIP Hollow out lime halves and
serve sorbet in them! Slice off a small
piece of the underside of each lime half so
they stand on their own without tipping. Use
a small cookie scoop or spoon to fill them.
Freeze for 30 minutes if necessary before
serving.

banana-berry split

PREP TIME
10 minutes

SERVES
4

4 bananas

16 ounces vanilla yogurt, divided

½ cup chocolate chips or chocolate shavings

1 cup blueberries or your favorite berry

Chocolate sauce or caramel sauce, for drizzling

Multicolored sprinkles/jimmies, for garnish

Assemble the splits and serve.
Peel the bananas and halve them lengthwise. In each of 4 bowls, position 2 banana halves side by side, spoon ½ cup of the yogurt over top of each, and sprinkle each with the chocolate chips and berries. Drizzle with chocolate and/or caramel sauce, dust with colorful sprinkles/jimmies, and serve.

DID YOU KNOW? Rubbing the inside of a banana peel on a bug bite, poison ivy, or poison oak will help relieve itching and inflammation.

frozen s'mores hot chocolate

PREP TIME
20 minutes

COOK TIME
5 minutes

SERVES
4

**TOOLS/
EQUIPMENT**
2 shallow bowls
4 glasses
Mixer
Small saucepan
or pot
Blender

3 full sheets graham crackers

8 tablespoons hot fudge topping

8 tablespoons marshmallow creme

1 cup heavy (whipping) cream

5 ounces semi-sweet chocolate chips

¼ cup sugar

1½ tablespoons cocoa powder

2 cups whole milk, divided

4 cups crushed ice

Prepare the graham crackers.
Break one full sheet of graham crackers into 4 even pieces, and set aside. Break the remaining 2 sheets of graham crackers into smaller pieces and set in a shallow bowl.

Prepare the glasses.
Put the hot fudge topping in a shallow bowl. Dip the rims of 4 glasses into the hot fudge topping, then roll the rims in the graham cracker pieces.

Decorate the glasses.
Dribble 2 tablespoons of marshmallow creme around the inside of each glass. Then drizzle 2 tablespoons of hot fudge inside each glass. Refrigerate the glasses until you are ready for them.

Whip the cream.
Using a mixer, whip the heavy cream until stiff peaks form, about 4 minutes. Refrigerate until ready to use.

Melt the chocolate.
In a small saucepan over medium-low heat, combine the chocolate chips, sugar, cocoa powder, and 1 cup of milk. Stir until the chocolate is melted and smooth but not boiling. Remove from the heat and let cool slightly.

Blend the ingredients.
In a blender, combine the crushed ice, remaining 1 cup of milk, and cooled chocolate mixture. Blend until smooth, then pour into the prepared glasses.

Garnish and serve.
Spoon the whipped cream on top, then garnish each with a graham cracker piece. Enjoy immediately.

sautéed apples

PREP TIME
10 minutes

COOK TIME
25 minutes

SERVES
4 TO **6**

**TOOLS/
EQUIPMENT**
Cutting board
Knife
Large sauté pan
Wooden spoon
Small mason jars
or serving bowls

2½ tablespoons butter

6 firm, tart apples, such as Granny Smith or Honeycrisp, peeled and cut into small cubes

¾ cup brown sugar

½ cup chopped walnuts or raisins (or both)

1½ teaspoons ground cinnamon

½ teaspoon ground nutmeg

Pinch salt

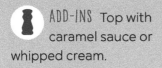 ADD-INS Top with caramel sauce or whipped cream.

Cook the apples.

In a large sauté pan over medium-low heat, melt the butter. Add the apples and brown sugar and sauté, stirring often, for 15 minutes, or until the apples are soft (see Troubleshooting).

Add the extras.

Add the walnuts and/or raisins, cinnamon, nutmeg, and salt. Stir to mix well, and sauté for an additional 6 to 8 minutes, or until thickened.

Serve.

Remove from the heat, spoon into small mason jars or serving bowls, and serve.

TROUBLESHOOTING Since the water content in apples may vary, if the apples become too sticky before softening, add an additional ½ tablespoon of butter.

DID YOU KNOW? More than 2,500 varieties of apples are grown in the United States. How many varieties have *you* tried?

strawberry granita

PREP TIME
10 minutes, plus
about 1 hour
30 minutes
to freeze

SERVES
4

**TOOLS/
EQUIPMENT**

Cutting board

Paring knife

Microplane
or zester

Food processor or
high-powered
blender

Medium bowl

13-by-9-inch pan
or metal bowl

Fork

Small glasses
or bowls

3 cups cleaned and hulled strawberries

1 teaspoon lemon zest

1 cup hot water

½ cup sugar

2 tablespoons freshly squeezed
lemon juice

Purée the berries.

In a food processor or high-powered blender,
purée the berries until smooth. Mix in the zest and
set aside.

Mix the granita.

In a medium bowl, combine the hot water, sugar, and
lemon juice, and stir until the sugar is dissolved. Add
the strawberry mixture to the sugar mixture, and
stir to combine.

Freeze the granita and serve.

Pour the mixture into a 13-by-9-inch pan or a
metal bowl, and place in the freezer for 30 minutes.
Remove from the freezer (edges should be icy),
and stir up the granita with a fork, moving the icy
parts to the center of the bowl as you do. Return
the granita to the freezer, and repeat the process
two more times (30 minutes apart each time). Once
the granita is dry and frozen, scrape with a fork into
small glasses or bowls and serve immediately.

 PRO TIP To wow your guests, garnish
these with mint leaves and/or berries.

roasted strawberry parfait

PREP TIME
15 minutes

COOK TIME
15 minutes

SERVES
4

TOOLS/ EQUIPMENT

Cutting board

Paring knife

Baking sheet

Parchment paper or silicone baking mat

Large bowl

Mixer

4 small glasses

2 cups fresh strawberries, hulled and quartered

1½ tablespoons brown sugar

1 cup mascarpone cheese

1 cup plain Greek yogurt

2 tablespoons honey

½ tablespoon freshly squeezed lemon juice

ADD-INS Try adding some granola, toasted coconut, or chocolate shavings.

Preheat the oven.

Preheat the oven to 425°F. Line a baking sheet with parchment paper or a silicone baking mat.

Prepare the strawberries.

In a large bowl, toss the berries with the brown sugar. Spread the berries evenly on the prepared baking sheet, and roast for 10 to 15 minutes, just until the berries begin to release their juices.

Make the yogurt mixture.

Meanwhile, use a mixer to whip the mascarpone cheese for 1 minute on high. Add the yogurt, honey, and lemon juice, and mix until just combined.

Assemble the parfaits and serve.

Into each of 4 small glasses, spoon a layer of yogurt. Top with the berries. Repeat the layers, ending with berries on top, and serve.

PRO TIP For an elegant presentation, garnish with mint leaves, a basil leaf, or some lemon zest.

TRY INSTEAD You can also serve this as a yogurt bowl. Just scoop the yogurt mixture into shallow bowls and decorate the tops with the berries.

cheesecake-stuffed strawberries

PREP TIME
25 minutes

SERVES
6+

TOOLS/ EQUIPMENT

Paper towel

Cutting board

Paring knife

Stand or hand mixer

Spatula

Piping bag with tip or plastic baggie

1 pound fresh strawberries, rinsed and patted dry

1 (8-ounce) block cream cheese, softened

½ cup powdered sugar

1 teaspoon vanilla extract

TRY INSTEAD If you would like a flavored cheesecake filling, swap the vanilla for 2 tablespoons freshly squeezed lemon juice or freshly squeezed orange juice.

Prepare the strawberries.
Using a paring knife, remove the stems from the strawberries. Cut a small piece off the bottom tip of each berry so the berry will stand on its own. Core the strawberries by cutting a circular opening into the berry, making a small hollow.

Mix the filling.
With a mixer, mix the cream cheese, powdered sugar, and vanilla until smooth, creamy, and fluffy, about 2 minutes.

Stuff the berries and serve.
Gently pat the berry openings with a paper towel. Spoon the cream cheese mixture into a piping bag or plastic baggie with a corner snipped off. Stuff the berries with the cream cheese mixture. Serve or refrigerate until ready to serve.

ADD-INS To dress these treats up, place one blueberry atop each stuffed berry, dust stuffed berries with graham cracker or sandwich cookie crumbs, or drizzle with a bit of melted chocolate.

HELPFUL HINTS These are best served the day you make them. You may have extra filling left over, depending on the size of the berries and how big each opening is. You can stuff additional berries or use leftovers as a dip with fruit.

lemon-blueberry shortbread tart

PREP TIME
10 minutes

COOK TIME
1 hour 5 minutes,
plus 1 hour
15 minutes to
rest and cool

SERVES

6+

**TOOLS/
EQUIPMENT**

Knife

8- or 9-inch
springform pan

Rimmed
baking sheet

Pastry cutter
(optional)

2 medium bowls

Whisk

Toothpick
(optional)

Mesh strainer
(optional)

FOR THE CRUST
Nonstick cooking spray

14 tablespoons cold butter,
cut into ½-inch cubes

1½ cups all-purpose flour

½ cup sugar

FOR THE CUSTARD
2½ cups fresh blueberries

3 large eggs

¾ cup granulated sugar

Juice of 2 large lemons

¼ cup all-purpose flour

¼ cup powdered sugar

Preheat the oven.
Preheat the oven to 400°F. Spray an 8- or 9-inch springform pan with cooking spray. Place the pan on a rimmed baking sheet.

Make the crust.
In a medium bowl, combine the butter, flour, and sugar. Use a pastry cutter or clean fingers to cut in the butter until the mixture forms coarse crumbs. Press the crust mixture into the bottom of the prepared pan. Bake for 16 to 20 minutes, or just until the crust begins to turn lightly golden in color. Remove from the oven and reduce the temperature to 325°F.

Reduce the oven temperature.
Reduce the oven temperature to 325°F.

Prepare the filling.
Scatter the blueberries over the crust. In a medium bowl, whisk the eggs and granulated sugar until thick and frothy, about 2 minutes. Add the lemon juice and flour, and whisk until blended and smooth. Pour the custard mixture over the crust with the blueberries.

Bake the tart.
Bake until the custard is set, 35 to 45 minutes (see Helpful Hints on the next page). It is done if it jiggles only slightly when the pan is shaken a bit, and the center is not wet. »

PRO TIPS Place the powdered sugar in a mesh strainer and tap the sides to make it "snow" powdered sugar. If you have leftovers, refresh the tart with additional powdered sugar the next time you want to enjoy a slice.

TRY INSTEAD You can also make this tart with raspberries.

Rest the tart.

Allow the tart to rest for 15 minutes. Run a sharp knife gently around the crust, then slowly release the pan. After you see that the sides have released, close the pan back up and allow to cool for an hour at room temperature. Chill in the refrigerator until ready to serve.

Garnish and serve.

Just before serving, use a mesh strainer to dust the tart with powdered sugar.

HELPFUL HINTS An 8-inch pan will take longer to set than a 9-inch pan (the deeper the custard, the longer the cook time). The custard should not brown. Also, you can process the butter, flour, and sugar in a food processor, pulsing until coarse crumbs are formed.

marble cookies

PREP TIME
15 minutes

COOK TIME
10 minutes

SERVES
6+

1¾ cups all-purpose flour, divided

¼ teaspoon salt

1 teaspoon baking soda

2 sticks butter, softened

¾ cup granulated sugar

¾ cup brown sugar

2 large eggs

1 teaspoon vanilla extract

6 tablespoons cocoa powder

1 cup chocolate sprinkles/jimmies

 PRO TIP Get creative when you combine the light and dark doughs. Swirl them around a bit to make fun color shapes.

Preheat the oven.

Preheat the oven to 375°F, and line a baking sheet with parchment paper or a silicone baking mat.

Mix the dry ingredients.

In a medium bowl, combine 1¼ cups of flour, salt, and baking soda. Set aside.

Mix the wet ingredients.

In a large bowl, combine the butter, granulated sugar, and brown sugar, and mix until smooth. Add the eggs and vanilla, and mix until blended. Add the flour and baking soda mixture, and mix until smooth and creamy.

Prepare the dough.

Divide the dough in half, placing one half into the medium bowl you used for the flour mixture and the other half in another medium bowl. Add the remaining ½ cup of flour to one batch of dough, and the cocoa powder to the other batch. Mix both doughs until smooth and creamy. Scoop the light dough into balls about the size of a walnut and place on a piece of parchment paper. Repeat with the chocolate dough.

Shape and bake.

Take one of each color ball of dough, press together and flatten so that one side is half light and the other is half dark. Roll the edges liberally in the chocolate sprinkles. Place on the baking sheet 1 inch apart, and bake for 11 minutes. Don't let the edges brown.

Cool and enjoy.

Let the cookies cool for a few minutes, and then, using a cookie spatula, transfer them to a cooling rack until completely cool. Store in an airtight container.

lemon soufflés

PREP TIME
20 minutes

COOK TIME
20 minutes

SERVES
6

**TOOLS/
EQUIPMENT**

Microplane
or zester

6 (8-ounce)
ramekins

Baking sheet

3 small bowls

Heavy saucepan

Medium bowl

Whisk

Knife

Mesh strainer

2 tablespoons butter, softened

5 tablespoons granulated sugar, divided

3 large egg yolks, plus 5 large egg whites

1 cup milk

1 tablespoon vanilla extract

¼ cup all-purpose flour

4 tablespoons freshly squeezed lemon juice, plus 2 tablespoons lemon zest, finely grated

1 tablespoon powdered sugar, plus more for dusting

Preheat the oven.
Preheat the oven to 400°F.

Prepare the ramekins.
Using your fingertips, coat 6 (8-ounce) ramekins with the butter. Dust the ramekins with 2 table-spoons of granulated sugar, rolling it around the sides and emptying the excess out into the next ramekin. Place the ramekins on a baking sheet in the refrigerator to chill.

Separate the eggs.
Separate the eggs, placing the yolks in one small bowl and egg whites in another. Chill the egg whites until ready to use.

Heat the milk.
In a heavy saucepan, bring the milk to a boil. Remove from the heat.

Mix the ingredients.
In a medium bowl, whisk together the egg yolks, vanilla, and 1 tablespoon of granulated sugar. Whisk in the flour. Whisk ¼ cup of the hot milk into the egg yolk mixture until blended. Continue mixing the hot milk into the egg yolk mixture, ¼ cup at a time, until all the milk is incorporated.

Thicken the mixture.
Pour the mixture back into the saucepan, and stir constantly over medium-low heat until thickened, about 2 minutes, moving the pot on and off the heat as you do so the mixture does not get too hot. If clumps begin to form, remove from the heat and whisk vigorously to smooth it out (see Trouble-shooting). Remove the custard from the heat.

Mix the lemon.
In a small bowl, mix together the lemon zest, lemon juice, and powdered sugar, and then add to the custard, whisking until smooth.

Beat the egg whites.
Beat the egg whites on high speed until they hold soft peaks. Sprinkle the remaining 2 tablespoons of granulated sugar over the egg whites, and beat until stiff and shiny. Fold ¼ of the egg whites into the custard until the whites disappear. Fold in the remaining egg whites until just blended; don't over blend or you'll deflate the egg whites and the batter will turn soupy.

Fill the ramekins.
Spoon the batter into the ramekins, filling just to the top. Level the tops with a knife. Use your finger to go around the inside perimeter of each ramekin to clean the edges.

Bake the soufflés.
Reduce the oven temperature to 375°F, and immediately place the ramekins in the oven on a baking sheet. Bake until puffed and the tops turn golden brown, 12 to 14 minutes. They should still be wobbly; move them slowly and carefully.

Garnish and serve.
Use a small mesh strainer to sprinkle with powdered sugar and enjoy immediately.

flourless chocolate cake

PREP TIME
15 minutes

COOK TIME
45 minutes,
plus 15 minutes
to cool

SERVES
6

TOOLS/
EQUIPMENT
8- or 9-inch round
springform pan or
cake pan
Parchment paper
or wax paper
Cutting board
Knife
Large metal bowl
Small pot
Spatula
Whisk
Toothpick

Nonstick cooking spray

8 ounces dark chocolate (60% cacao)

2 sticks butter

1 teaspoon vanilla extract

1 cup plus 2 tablespoons sugar

6 large eggs (or 5 extra-large eggs)

1 cup unsweetened cocoa powder

Prepare the pan.
Preheat the oven to 375°F. Prepare an 8- or 9-inch springform pan or round cake pan by spraying the inside of the pan with cooking spray then lining the bottom with parchment or wax paper cut into a circle to fit the bottom of the pan. Spray the paper after you place it in the pan.

Break the chocolate.
Break the chocolate apart into small ½-inch pieces, and place in a large metal bowl. Cut the butter into ½-inch chunks and add to the same bowl.

Melt the chocolate.
Fill a small pot halfway with water and bring to a simmer. Carefully place the metal bowl with the chocolate and butter on top of the pot, and allow the mixture to begin melting. First stir with a spatula, and then as it melts, whisk to incorporate it (see Helpful Hint on the next page).

Add the remaining ingredients.
Once the mixture is melted and smooth, remove from the heat and whisk in the vanilla and sugar. Whisk in the eggs, two at a time, until incorporated. Spoon in the cocoa powder, folding it in with a spatula until just combined. Scrape the batter into the prepared pan, smoothing evenly. Alternatively, hold both sides of the pan and hit it flat against the counter to help the batter even out. »

HELPFUL HINT To melt the chocolate and butter in the microwave, place the chocolate and butter in a large, microwave-safe bowl. Melt the chocolate and butter in the microwave for 1 minute. Remove and stir with a spatula or spoon for 1 minute. Allow it to sit for a minute, and stir again. If pieces of chocolate remain, microwave for another 15 seconds, then stir until smooth, repeating if necessary, for 15 seconds at a time, until smooth.

Bake and cool.
Bake for 35 to 45 minutes, or until the top of the cake crisps up and a toothpick inserted comes out mostly clean. Allow to cool for 15 minutes. If using a springform pan, release the sides and invert the cake carefully onto a plate. Remove the bottom of the pan and paper lining. Allow to cool. If using a cake pan, run a butter knife around the sides of the pan. Invert the pan onto a plate, carefully pull off the paper lining, and allow the cake to cool completely.

PRO TIP You can serve this cake as is, with a dusting of powdered sugar, or with some fresh whipped cream spread over top. Decorate with a small pile of chopped strawberries or your favorite small berries in the center or any way you choose.

chocolate & peanut butter squares

PREP TIME
5 minutes, plus
3 hours and
15 minutes
to chill

COOK TIME
10 minutes

SERVES
6

**TOOLS/
EQUIPMENT**

9-by-9-inch
baking pan

Parchment paper
or wax paper

Microwave-
safe dish

Spatula

Small saucepan

Whisk

1 pound white chocolate, chopped
or broken into pieces

1 cup peanut butter

1½ cups chocolate chips

½ cup heavy (whipping) cream

Prep the pan.
Line a 9-by-9-inch pan with parchment or wax
paper, leaving an overhang.

Melt the white chocolate.
In a microwave-safe dish, melt the white chocolate
in the microwave in 30-second increments, stirring
between cook times, until the white chocolate is
melted and creamy, but being careful not to overcook. Add the peanut butter and stir until blended
and smooth. Spread the mixture into the prepared
baking pan. Refrigerate for 15 minutes, or until a
bit firm.

Melt the milk chocolate.
In a small saucepan over medium-high heat, combine the chocolate chips and cream and heat until
melted and smooth, stirring constantly. Do not allow
the mixture to boil. Pour over the peanut butter
mixture.

Chill and cut.
Chill for at least 3 hours or overnight. Later, lift out
the candy, cut into small squares, and serve.

HELPFUL HINT These make a great
holiday, Valentine's Day, or birthday gift.
Use a small tin or box lined with tissue paper.
Place a pretty ribbon around it and attach the
recipe, and you have a great homemade gift!

MEASUREMENT CONVERSIONS

Volume Equivalents (Liquid)

US STANDARD	US STANDARD (OUNCES)	METRIC (APPROXIMATE)
2 tablespoons	1 fl. oz.	30 mL
¼ cup	2 fl. oz.	60 mL
½ cup	4 fl. oz.	120 mL
1 cup	8 fl. oz.	240 mL
1½ cups	12 fl. oz.	355 mL
2 cups or 1 pint	16 fl. oz.	475 mL
4 cups or 1 quart	32 fl. oz.	1 L
1 gallon	128 fl. oz.	4 L

Oven Temperatures

FAHRENHEIT (F)	CELSIUS (C) (APPROXIMATE)
250°F	120°C
300°F	150°C
325°F	165°C
350°F	180°C
375°F	190°C
400°F	200°C
425°F	220°C
450°F	230°C

Volume Equivalents (Dry)

US STANDARD	METRIC (APPROXIMATE)
⅛ teaspoon	0.5 mL
¼ teaspoon	1 mL
½ teaspoon	2 mL
¾ teaspoon	4 mL
1 teaspoon	5 mL
1 tablespoon	15 mL
¼ cup	59 mL
⅓ cup	79 mL
½ cup	118 mL
⅔ cup	156 mL
¾ cup	177 mL
1 cup	235 mL
2 cups or 1 pint	475 mL
3 cups	700 mL
4 cups or 1 quart	1 L

Weight Equivalents

US STANDARD	METRIC (APPROXIMATE)
½ ounce	15 g
1 ounce	30 g
2 ounces	60 g
4 ounces	115 g
8 ounces	225 g
12 ounces	340 g
16 ounces or 1 pound	455 g

RECIPE INDEX

INDEX

·················

ACKNOWLEDGMENTS

To Connor, my first mini sous chef and taste-tester extraordinaire. You showed me that cooking with my kids was fun and inspired so many food memories (and my first cookbook). Watching you get excited by food always makes me happy! ILY!

To Samantha, my partner in crime in cooking, baking, and *Master Chef*–watching, *and* the best hand model around, lol! Your spot-on palate amazes me. I am excited for the day we'll be cooking in your kitchen (*though I am in no rush for you to grow up*). Thank you for *always* helping me when I need it in the kitchen and beyond . . . *Peem*!

To John, my original hand model (who knew?). Thanks for giving me the initial push and the opportunity to spread my wings and follow my passion.

To my mom, dad, grandmom, and grammy, it is because of each of you, your signature recipes, everyday meals, and baked goods that I became the passionate cook I am today. Food memories are the BEST memories!

To Skylar, for always wanting to jump in and help cook or bake, and to Anita for always being willing to help out. Thank you!

To Janet, my first foodie friend. Finding a kindred spirit who was as excited about cooking as I was felt amazing and inspired me to be more adventurous in the kitchen. Lucky me!

To the first chefs I ever saw on TV (*thank you PBS*); Jacques Pépin, Justin Wilson, and Martin Yan . . . I thought you were talking to *me*! You each were *so* fun to watch; thank you for igniting my passion for all things food at a young age and for paving the way for today's celebrity chefs.

To the Callisto Team, thank you for your support and vision in bringing this cookbook to life! I hope that tweens, teens, and even adults who are newer to cooking enjoy the recipes in this book.

To anyone (*no matter your age*) who may think they can't cook (or hasn't really tried): If you can read . . . you can cook. Go for it; it's delicious!

ABOUT THE AUTHOR

Colleen Kennedy is the creator of the popular food blog Souffle Bombay (SouffleBombay.com), where she shares creative recipes that are easy enough for anyone to make to wow their friends and family. Colleen's work has appeared in various print, online, and television outlets. Follow Colleen on Facebook, Twitter, Pinterest, and Instagram for new recipes, tips, and more @SouffleBombay.

discover more in the
kid chef
series

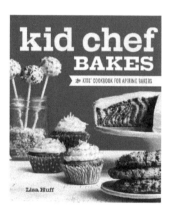

Kid Chef
The Foodie Kids' Cookbook:
Healthy Recipes and Culinary
Skills for the New Cook
in the Kitchen

Melina Hammer

978-1-94345-120-3

$15.99 US / $19.99 CAN

Kid Chef Bakes
The Kids' Cookbook
for Aspiring Bakers

Lisa Huff

978-1-62315-942-9

$14.99 US / $19.99 CAN

Kid Chef Junior
My First Kids' Cookbook

Anjali Shah

978-1-64152-135-2

$14.99 US / $19.99 CAN

CPSIA information can be obtained
at www.ICGtesting.com
Printed in the USA
LVHW051731271118
597925LV00001BA/1/P